The Last Stronghold

Scottish Gaelic Traditions
of Newfoundland

Margaret Bennett

First published in 1989
by Breakwater Books, Canada.
First published in Great Britain
by Canongate Publishing Limited,
17 Jeffrey Street, Edinburgh.

© 1989 Margaret Bennett

British Library Cataloguing in Publication Data
Bennett, Margaret, 1946-
The last stronghold: Scottish Newfoundlanders.
1. Newfoundland. Codroy region. Scottish communities
I. Title
305.8'9136'0718

ISBN 0 86241 197 1

*Photographs used throughout this book
are the property of the MacArthur Family,
and are reproduced here by kind permission of
Margaret Cormeir, Frank MacArthur, and George MacArthur.*

Cover illustration by Alan McGowan

Typeset and designed by Breakwater Books
Printed in Canada

to the memory of
Mary and Allan MacArthur
who upheld the Gaelic language and traditions
– the heritage of their own people

THE CODROY VALLEY

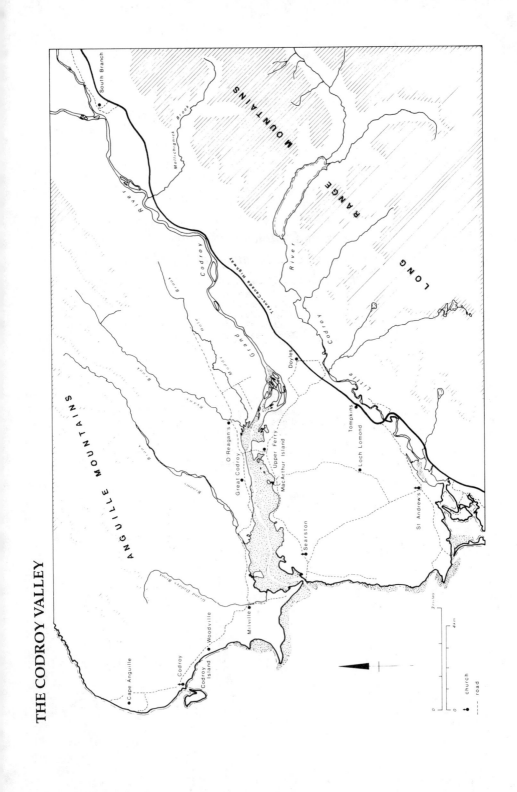

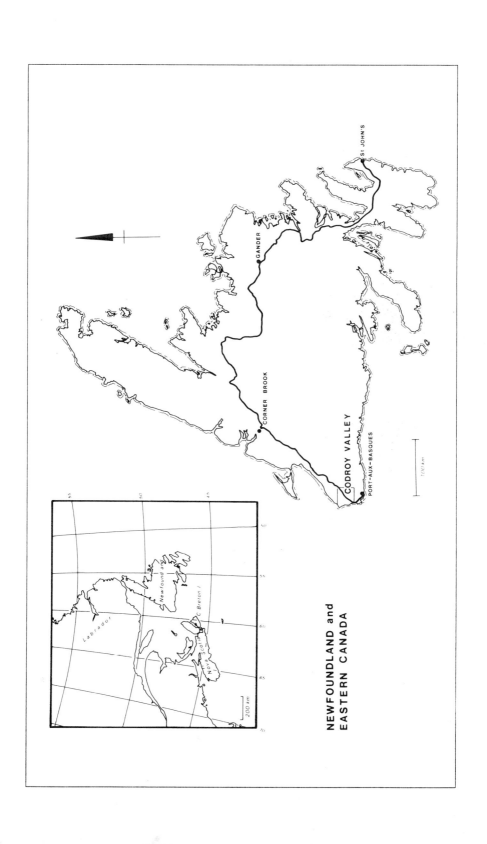

NEWFOUNDLAND and
EASTERN CANADA

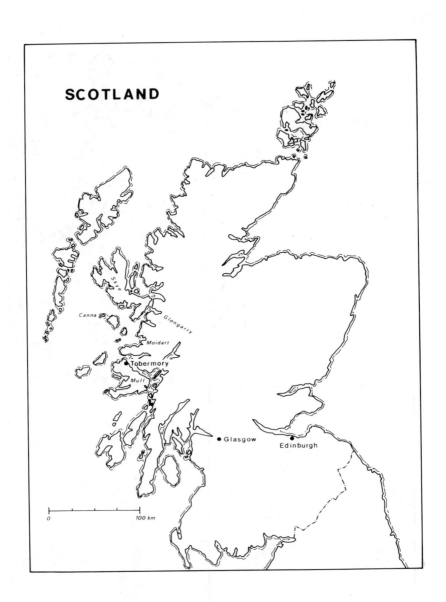

SCOTLAND

Skye

Canna

Glengarry

Moidart

Tobermory

Mull

Glasgow

Edinburgh

0   100 km

Contents

Acknowledgements

In preparing this book, I have incurred a great debt of gratitude to many people in various parts of Newfoundland and Scotland. It is with pleasure, then, that I acknowledge their important contribution to the finished work.

My thanks go back over several decades: the earliest to my parents, Peigi and George Bennett, who brought me up on the Isles of Skye and Lewis, where my earliest appreciation of the culture of the Scottish Gaels was nurtured. My mother's Gaelic songs and my father's bagpipe music were part of our daily existence, and no doubt influenced me from the earliest age. When I was in my late teens (and had left home) my father decided to work in Newfoundland. The move aroused my curiosity and prompted me to visit the province which was later to become my home for several years. Then, by coincidence, my parents settled only eighty miles from my area of research, and as a result they unwittingly made an invaluable contribution to my work. Their occasional visits to the Codroy Valley and the ease with which they participated in the general conversation, songs, and music undoubtedly elicited much of the material contained here. Special thanks go to my mother who, with endless patience, later helped with my enormous task of transcribing field tapes.

Gratitude is also due to my grandparents, the late John and Flora Stewart of Glenconon, Skye, whose croft was my second home. There, from earliest childhood, I was given a clearer understanding of many aspects of the way of life of our people, not only from their own day (the early 1880s to the early 1970s) but from much earlier family traditions.

I also appreciated having my twin sisters, Marie and Florence, both nurses, and my brother-in-law, Dr. David Clow (Florence's husband) accompany me on a few visits to the Codroy Valley. Their interest in medicine brought out some interesting aspects of the way of life in the early days before there was any medical service in the area.

I wish to acknowledge and thank several sources of assistance at Memorial University of Newfoundland. First and foremost, I am deeply grateful to my supervisor of studies, Professor Herbert Halpert, whose wealth of experience in folklore fieldwork and extensive knowledge of the subject was an inspiration to me. Always accessible, he was my main source of guidance and advice which he freely gave with endless patience and enthusiasm.

My thanks also go to John Mannion of the Geography Department, to John D.A. Widdowson of the Folklore Department (and of Sheffield University), and to Miss Agnes O'Dea, head of the Centre for Newfoundland Studies at the Queen Elizabeth II Library, Memorial University of Newfoundland, who gave me invaluable assistance in locating documentation from published sources. Appreciation is also due to the library staff in general who were always ready to give assistance when it was requested.

I wish to thank Memorial University of Newfoundland for providing me with a University fellowship during my first two years as a post-graduate student. This facilitated the major part of my research in the Codroy Valley.

For the photographs and graphics in this book I am indebted to the MacArthur family for their kind permission to have the family album photographed, for additional details, and for permission to publish the photos. Thanks also to friends and technical staff at Memorial University of Newfoundland and Edinburgh University for help in obtaining and processing maps, photographs and graphics.

Over the years of my association with the Codroy Valley, I have been continually aware of the debt of gratitude I owe to so many people there. My deepest appreciation goes first to the late Allan and Mary MacArthur, without whom this book would have been impossible. They warmly welcomed me into their home and extended their hospitality over the many months I spent with them. They generously shared their wealth of knowledge of the Scottish Newfoundlanders with me and instructed me on a great diversity of topics. On many occasions they took me and showed me, or demonstrated certain skills so that I should be able to see for myself what they were describing. In short, they made me part of a large, extended family.

Consequently I would like to thank the entire MacArthur family, including the MacIsaac and MacNeil branches of it, and also close friends such as the late George and Lucy Cormier, the late Con Gabriel and his wife, Rita; the Gales and the O'Quinns of Millville; Father R. White and Father D. Gash, and all others who offered me friendship and kindness while I lived in the Valley.

Special thanks go to Frank and Margaret MacArthur, who corresponded regularly with me in Scotland and who were a generous and invaluable source of information in more recent years, and to Margaret (nee MacArthur), her husband Leo Cormier and their family, whose warmth and hospitality were constantly appreciated.

Also in Newfoundland, I was grateful for the friendship and encouragement of Cathy and Lloyd Leland; Hilda and Murdo Murray; and Kate Evans.

In Edinburgh, where I wrote the book (based on an academic thesis), I also incurred a debt of gratitude. I wish to acknowledge with thanks the Faculty of Arts of Edinburgh University, who helped to finance a consultation at Memorial University of Newfoundland, and the typing of the manuscript for publication.

I am grateful to the Carnegie Trust to the Universities of Scotland whose financial assistance supported the final stage of research.

I would like to thank Dr. John Lorne Campbell of Canna who permitted me to use information from his own admirable research.

During preparation for publication I was extremely fortunate in being able to draw upon the invaluable resources, skills and advice of my colleagues at the School of Scottish Studies, Edinburgh University. Special thanks go to John MacInnes, Gaelic scholar and wordsmith, who carefully read the entire manuscript and made last-minute suggestions which undoubtedly sharpened the focus of some of the pictures I wish to portray; and to Morag MacLeod, who patiently listened to my tapes and went over the song texts, generously giving of her time and expertise in that area. Donald Archie MacDonald, Alan Bruford and Peter Cooke also lent an ear when my own could not discern the finer points of Gaelic or intricacies of canntaireachd. Special thanks go to Tom Burton, Irene Riggs, and Marie and Bill Salton for help in revising the proofs.

I am eternally grateful to Joan MacKenzie of the School of Scottish Studies who not only typed the entire manuscript, but inspired me to press on toward completion. Her patience and good humour, especially during the final stages of corrections, were more than encouraging to me.

Finally, my warm appreciation goes to my son, Martyn, my constant companion during his first four years, much of which was spent in the Codroy Valley. With his childish curiosity and enthusiasm, he arranged for me to share with him the delights of exploring the barns and stables, feeding the animals, riding on top of hay carts; and when he and his good friend, George MacArthur, had harnessed the horse and sleigh, they agreed to take me with them through the snow on the winter wood-cutting trip they had planned. Throughout his seventeen years, he has had a life-long affection for the Codroy Valley. Martyn has made a substantial contribution to this book by transcribing the melodies of all the songs, and shares my hope that young people will, for many years, enjoy the folk culture and music of the Scottish Newfoundlanders.

Introduction

Back again! Just like the rest of us, can't stay
away, b'y! But what in the world made you
come here in the first place?
Angus McNeill,
Codroy Valley, July 1986

I first became interested in the Scots of the Codroy Valley just one
week after arriving in Newfoundland in August 1968. At the time,
I was staying with my father in a motel about a hundred miles from
St. John's. As a new immigrant to Canada from the Scottish Hebrides,
I was surprised to hear from my father, also a Scottish immigrant,
that a native Newfoundlander who spoke Gaelic and had a background very similar to my own was staying in the same motel. About
sixty years old, the late Hector MacIsaac was at the time working as
a water engineer some five hundred miles from his home in St.
Andrews, which is in the Codroy Valley on the west coast of Newfoundland. He and my father had become acquaintances and had
discovered that they had common roots, my father having been born
and raised in Scotland and MacIsaac's people coming from Scotland
three generations back.

The meeting with Hector MacIsaac was a memorable one. There
were no formal introductions; he was simply pointed out to me
across a room. Unobserved, I went up to him and greeted him in
Gaelic. He responded with great delight, shaking my hand all the
time he spoke, scarcely believing that there was any young person
left with a knowledge of his mother tongue. He said that all the
younger generation of the Codroy Valley learned English as their

first language, and now even the old people who had spoken nothing but Gaelic in their youth had very little opportunity of speaking the language. Little did I realize that this first meeting would lead me to these 'old people', especially to an outstanding tradition-bearer whose wealth of knowledge was to hold my interest and affection for many years to come.

Hector MacIsaac described to me his home community, his Gaelic-speaking family, and the Scottish Gaels who inhabited his native part of Newfoundland. The Valley, as he called the area, seemed unique in Newfoundland in terms of language and culture, as it is in fact the only area of its kind in the province where many of the earlier settlers were Gaelic-speaking Cape Breton Scots.

My initial interest in the Codroy Valley was revived about a year later when I saw in the TV section of a newspaper the photograph of a piper with the caption "Cameras visit Codroy Valley." I watched the programme, a half-hour documentary film illustrating features of the traditional way of life of the English, French and Scots who settled there, along with camera shots of the picturesque scenery. What I saw and heard, and particularly the pipe music and Gaelic songs, made such an impression upon me that I took a clipping from the newspaper and, for the only time in my life, I determined that I would go and visit someone I had seen on television, namely the Codroy Valley Scottish piper, Allan MacArthur.

I was then very much encouraged by two events. Firstly, my parents moved out to the west coast of Newfoundland to a place only eighty miles from the Codroy Valley; and secondly, I approached Professor Herbert Halpert, head of the Folklore Department at Memorial University of Newfoundland, to discuss a possible project. He advised me to enrol in the graduate studies programme in Folklore where I could pursue my interest in greater depth and with all the facilities of that department. Then, in a manner which I soon learned was characteristic of the man, Professor Halpert reached toward his enormous book collection and introduced me to the most up-to-date reference which cited the Codroy Valley. His "I'm sure you'll have read it already" was enough of a hint for me to make certain that I would comb the shelves of the University library for all available clues to the Scottish Newfoundlanders.

The newly-published book was *Newfoundland* by the well-known naturalist and writer Harold Horwood, whose family has been in Newfoundland for over three centuries. It was in reading Horwood's words that I understood Halpert's urgency, for this definitive (and indeed excellent) guide to the Province of Newfoundland had already, in 1969, pronounced one of its native languages *dead:*

This Land of Ours

Allan MacArthur, 85-year-old farmer and piper of Codroy Valley in western Newfoundland, plays for a group of youngsters and for viewers of CBC-TV's This Land of Our Series, in Valley of the Winds, Saturday at 7 p.m.

Cameras visit Codroy Valley

Saturday at 7 p.m. CBC cameras pay a visit to the Codroy Valley, in a program on This Land of Ours, entitled Valley of the Winds. The valley is one of the most picturesque farming areas in Newfoundland where the wind sometimes blows through at 100 miles per hour. It's an area where traditional methods are still used and where a way of life counts for something.

Viewers will meet Mrs. Emily McDougall, the valley's official "wind watcher". From her reports, the railway determines if it's safe to send rolling stock through the area, where on two past occasions high winds have blown trains right off the track.

Also seen on the program are Alf Gale, a farmer whose family was among the first settlers in Codroy Valley; and Allan MacArthur, an 85-year old farmer and valley piper. An old-time milling dance, put on specially for CBC is also shown. Host is John Foster.

The Evening Telegram, St. John's, Vol. 91, No. 27 (February 7, 1969), p. 15.
(Reproduced with permission of the Publisher.)

"When I was a young boy growing up beside this river," the old man said as we gazed out over the wide, meandering channels of the Codroy, "we were almost completely cut off from the world, but we lived very comfortably. It was a simple life, of course. We wove everything that we wore out of homespun from our own sheep, except for skin boots that we made ourselves, for the winter. There was plenty of good food: fresh salmon and smoked salmon and game, and we raised so many vegetables that we could trade or sell a lot of them to the ships that came to the Gulf to fish in the summer.

"We were a mixed-up lot, too. As you walked to church on Sunday morning you would hear people on the road speaking four languages: French, English, Micmac, and Gaelic, with French the commonest of all. But we got along well enough together. I don't remember a single feud or serious quarrel between people of different races, in my whole lifetime."

These languages have died out now. Gaelic is no longer spoken at all, French by only a few families on the most isolated part of Newfoundland's west coast, and Micmac by even fewer, in a cranny of Bay d'Espoir far off to the east.[1]

Died out? That was enough inspiration to set me off on the five hundred and twenty mile drive from St. John's to the Codroy Valley to visit these people who had already made such an impression upon me. On the way there I stopped at Stephenville to invite my mother to accompany me to the one place where she would be able to speak in her much-loved mother tongue. Fortunately, she accepted, in spite of her "You can't just walk up to their doors, can you?"

A sight-seeing drive through the Codroy Valley showed it to consist of a number of closely knit settlements, rather like the houses that are strung out along the country roadsides in rural Scotland, with one village merging into the next. On making this comparison I concluded that, "just like at home," people probably knew exactly who lived in every house of their community. Our first stop was the Grand Codroy Provincial Park, where the park attendant, the late Con Gabriel, looked at the newspaper clipping and listened to my quest. He said he would be more than pleased to have the opportunity of bringing some of Allan MacArthur's fellow Scots to visit the old man.

As Con predicted, Allan MacArthur was delighted to meet anyone from Scotland and particularly from one of the Gaelic-speaking areas of the Highlands and Islands that his mother and grandmother had so often told him about. A very alert man in his eighties, Allan talked spontaneously about his Scottish background. It was obvious at once that he was extremely proud of his ancestors and enjoyed having an audience with whom he could share his interest. He asked what Scotland was like now and referred to the things his people had told him about the country they left in the 1800s "when they sailed to America." In spite of the fact that he had never seen Scotland, he could tell me that "just about this time of year the hills of Scotland will be turning purple with heather—but there's no heather here." A hundred and forty years stood between Allan MacArthur and his grandmother's last sight of her beloved land, yet the picture in his mind was as sharply focused as my own year-old image.

If the television portrayal of Allan MacArthur impressed me, the man himself more than lived up to my expectations. Before long our *ceilidh* (visit) revealed that we had a common love for Gaelic songs and Scottish music, and that Allan MacArthur's musical background was very similar to my own. His mother had taught him many Gaelic songs, and he had learned to play the bagpipes from his uncle and other relatives. For my own part, I had been brought up on the Isle of Skye surrounded by music in a household where we, like the MacArthurs, made our own entertainment. My mother taught me many of her Gaelic songs and my father, a keen piper, influenced my great love for the bagpipes. Of equal influence were my maternal grandparents, John and Flora Stewart, in whose croft I spent every available week-end and holiday. There they fed my insatiable appetite for Gaelic tradition, an interest that not only remained after they had died but was to become foremost in my life. Little wonder, then, that I felt so much at home in the company of Allan MacArthur and his wife Mary, whose forebears were MacDonalds from Glengarry.

Allan and Mary
MacArthur, 1970

From that first visit it was quite clear that Allan MacArthur was more than the "farmer and piper" that the newspaper article had mentioned. He was a singer, accordionist, story-teller, historian, and craftsman into the bargain. We parted company, neither of us in any doubt that I would take the man at his word and come back again soon.

> Well, I would like to see you coming every week. I could keep
> you up all night telling you stories and singing you songs.

If the long, snowy Newfoundland winter permitted only one return visit to the MacArthurs, it nevertheless left ample time to read and to plan. The main intention was to compile a collection of Scottish Newfoundland folklore and oral history. The latter could be set beside the written history to make a composite picture of the settlement of the Scots in the Codroy Valley, for the standard textbooks give only sketchy descriptions. Fortunately, the University's Centre for Newfoundland Studies had the invaluable expertise of its head, Miss Agnes O'Dea, who was always ready to explain the subtleties of historical researching, and with her helpful advice a thorough search of the "Newfoundland Room" proved fruitful. Substantial relevant material turned up in the records kept by travellers, surveyors, geologists and clergy. Prominent among these were William Epps Cormack, who journeyed across Newfoundland in 1822; Archdeacon Wix, who kept a journal from his missionary visit to Newfoundland in 1835; geologist J.B. Jukes, who kept a record of his travels in Newfoundland in 1839 and 1840; and Bishop Feild, who came to the coastal Newfoundland settlements in 1849. Also dating back to the earliest years of settlement were newspapers, magazines and government documents, all containing occasional references to the Codroy Valley. In the Valley itself, the parish records kept by the local priest, Father R. White, were useful for details of certain dates.

Large as this body of material might be, I am convinced that this particular account would be meagre and lacking in vitality if I had depended upon these written sources alone. The historian Philip D. Jordan affirms that unless the historian is willing to look further than printed documents, he does not have the complete account of the history of a society. He suggests that traditional oral material can make a valuable contribution to the historian's understanding of the society he studies.[2] The folklorist, too, "can come to the aid of the historian, whose analysis of statistical data and historical documents seldom permits conclusions regarding the ways of life on a local level."[3]

> Rarely does an individual informant know all there is to be
> learned about specific historical occurrences. It is necessary to

query several people and collate their traditions before the complete picture can be seen.[4]

Summer arrived in the Codroy Valley, and so did I. Home was a thirty-foot trailer, situated across the river from the MacArthurs, an ideal place from which to conduct fieldwork.

In a nucleus of settlements such as the Codroy Valley where people are naturally friendly, and some have obviously Scottish names, it was easy to find Scots settlers. By strange coincidence my own name, Bennett, a very common west coast of Newfoundland and Codroy Valley name, elicited its own local curiosity. Several Bennetts who had intermarried with Scots were mentioned, as were a few Gaelic speakers whose families had retained the original French form of Benoit rather than adopting the Anglicized version. Such changes were not generally made by choice, but were more often imposed by the early priests who had the curious habit of 'correcting' the spellings of French names: for example, a name like Au Coin must surely have been O'Quinn to the Irish priests. Today, many of the O'Quinns can, with pride (and a little indignation!) tell of their distinctly French background. Carried along by conversation topics such as these, and the unfailing helpfulness of local people, I found myself introduced to innumerable residents who were quick to learn of my background and my reason for coming to live in the Valley. With informants galore, it was indeed a folklorist's paradise!

Systematically I visited and enquired, placing emphasis upon the Gaelic traditions I wished to hear about. There was a definite awareness of the important place the Scots had in the Valley, and regardless of background, everyone seemed to know an occasional word of the old language. When asked for specific details, however, almost everyone interviewed responded by directing me to Allan MacArthur, whom they considered to be an authority on the Codroy Valley Scots. Not only was he considered the best source of information on the history of the Valley, but was also the recognized authority on the legends, songs, and general traditions of the area. I was soon to find out that he was unique: the last survivor to have such a wealth of knowledge about his cultural heritage. Over the years Allan MacArthur had come to earn great respect and admiration for his remarkable memory and his lively personality. Realizing that I had the good fortune of meeting with the last real stronghold of the Scottish Gaelic traditions of the Codroy Valley, I saw the urgency of trying to preserve as much as possible of Allan's recollections of early days of settlement in the Valley, along with his repertoire of songs and his memory of the old-time stories, cures and crafts that were all part of the way of life of the first Scottish settlers.

In his closing years, Allan knew all too well that the language he had grown up with and loved, along with the lore that had been handed down for centuries through Gaelic, were likely to disappear from the Valley with the passing of his own generation. It was perhaps not surprising, then, that Allan MacArthur welcomed the opportunity of having someone whom he could regard as another link in the chain of tradition-bearing, and having the advantage of a similar Highland background in a Gaelic-speaking area I became the repository he was looking for. He regarded the tape recorder that I brought to his house as a wonderful tool which could be used in this eleventh-hour effort to preserve some of his traditions and memories. There were many times in those pre-video days when I wished there could be some way of capturing Allan MacArthur's reactions as he listened to his own singing or pipe-playing played back on the tape recorder. At first he was amazed and somewhat amused at being able to listen to his own music; later, as he became more accustomed to the idea, he seemed quite convinced that this was a wonderful way of preserving all his songs which, at one time, he feared might have been lost forever.

His attitude to the recording of conversation was somewhat similar, and he firmly defended my use of it. Once, for example, when Mrs. MacArthur, slightly hesitant that the reminiscences of an old man should be recorded, reminded her husband of the presence of the tape recorder, he sat back and gently said that he was "only telling the truth." He said that they knew how things were in the Valley many years before because they had been born and brought up there; what happened before that was told to them by their parents and grandparents, so that also could be nothing other than the truth. On no occasion throughout my many visits did Allan lose any of his enthusiasm or willingness to tell the story of the Scottish Newfoundlanders.

To preserve the accuracy of his account I transcribed Allan MacArthur's own words from the tapes.[5] These transcriptions, however, can give only a pale reflection of the man himself. While the words convey the information to the reader, they cannot convey the slow, deliberate articulation of his soft-spoken Newfoundland-Scots accent, nor the warmth of the character of the man who spoke them. Not only is the printed page devoid of a means of indicating his vocal expression, there is also a total absence of his wonderful facial expressions—the wistfulness and nostalgia of the exile; the glint of excitement of the adventurer; the sparkle of the entertainer; and the twinkle in the eye of the man who knew exactly how to hold the attention and fascination of the audience. Such are the drawbacks of transcription. To those who knew him the print will automatically remind them of all these characteristics; to readers who did not have that privilege, however, it is my hope that they will gradually get to know this memorable tradition-bearer and enjoy his acquaintance.

CHAPTER 1

God's Little Acre

> Tha m'fhearann saidhbhir air gach taobh
> dhiom.
> [My land is prosperous on all sides of me.]
> —*from an old Gaelic song*

The Codroy Valley is located in the southwest corner of Newfoundland, nestled between the Cape Anguille Mountains and
the southern end of the Long Range Mountains. It is drained by two
rivers, the Grand Codroy and the Little Codroy. As they enter the
Gulf of St. Lawrence, both rivers have long sand spits which extend
across most of the mile-wide mouths of the rivers, leaving only a narrow opening for access to the sea. The Grand Codroy is a slow-flow-
ing river; its wide estuary extends approximately seven miles inland;
much of it silted up, leaving only a narrow channel of deep water
for navigation. Some thirty small islands are situated in the estuary
of the Grand Codroy.

To the present-day visitor who usually approaches via the Trans
Canada Highway, the name Codroy Valley might understandably
present some confusion as the community of Codroy is actually
situated outside the Valley. People living in the area who have grown
up with the local name insist that visitors call the entire area either
by the more formal name 'the Codroy Valley' or by the simpler, local
name 'the Valley'. The older resident will tell you as well that the two
rivers were not always known by the names Grand Codroy and Little
Codroy but were once known as Grand River and Little River.
Perhaps the relevance of the use of the name 'Codroy' can be seen
more clearly by looking at the history of the region.

While most people who go there today approach by land, this was not the case when the earliest settlers arrived. Until the 1820s the Codroy Valley had been approached only by sea, and it is in this fact that one might find the reason for the choice of name given to the entire valley. Records show that by the early 1820s the community of Codroy was well established as a fishing port and base of operation for the French fishery in the coastal waters from Cape Ray to Cape Anguille. Anyone approaching the Valley in those early days would do so by way of this established port of Codroy. This, then, may well be the reason why the entire valley came to be named the Codroy Valley.

Like the rest of Newfoundland, the Codroy Valley has a temperate marine climate. Situated on the west coast of the island, and consequently much closer to the land mass of Canada, it experiences greater extremes of temperature than does the rest of the province. Spring arrives late, and although the summers are generally the warmest in Newfoundland, from the farmer's point of view the growing season is short. The area has an annual rainfall of forty-seven inches.

Road and rail communications in the Valley mainly follow the river banks and the sea coast, a pattern which is not simple to describe but which can be easily followed by referring to the map [page 4]. The two river mouths are about five miles apart at the coast. Approximately five miles inland, where the two rivers are closest together, the minor roads join the main arterial road linking the Valley with the rest of Newfoundland—the Trans Canada Highway. Leaving the Valley the road continues southward for twenty-five miles until it reaches Port aux Basques, the point of departure for the ferry connecting Newfoundland to the mainland of Canada. The railway line follows a route which is very close to that of the Trans Canada Highway, and when it reaches the Valley there are two stations, one at Doyles and the other at St. Andrew's.

The local parish contained in the Codroy Valley is known as St. Anne's Parish. It is composed of several settlements or 'sections' situated mainly along the banks of the river, and connected to one another by a network of minor roads. Commencing with the section which is furthest inland and continuing along the south bank of the Grand Codroy River toward its mouth are the settlements of Codroy Pond, North Branch, Coal Brook (sometimes called Cold Brook), South Branch, Tompkins, Doyles, Upper Ferry, and Searston. Along the north bank of that river are O'Regans, Great Codroy, and Millville; and continuing beyond the river mouth, along the sea coast, are the villages of Woodville, Codroy, and Cape Anguille.

Between the two rivers is Loch Lomond, and at the mouth of Little Codroy is the settlement of St. Andrew's, once called 'Little River'.

In accordance with the old orientation to the sea, there were three churches which once stood as magnificent landmarks, easily seen in a seaward approach. These were the Anglican church at Codroy, the Roman Catholic church at Searston (demolished in the mid-1970s), and the Roman Catholic church at St. Andrew's.

To anyone familiar with what might be considered typical Newfoundland scenery—a splendid predominance of thick coniferous forests interspersed with ponds (lakes) and large areas of barrens—the Codroy Valley forms a noticeable contrast. There one finds large scenic areas of arable and pasture land in the Valley with the upper slopes of the hills richly wooded. When the area was settled in the nineteenth century the early settlers took it upon themselves to clear the growth of trees from large areas of land to allow them to cultivate the fertile valley soils. This land clearance still continues today and, encouraged by the fact that the Newfoundland government offers subsidies for every acre of land cleared, several of the farmers have undertaken land clearance on a large scale in order to expand their farms.

The agricultural areas of the Valley form a large patchwork of fenced fields. Until recently (the 1970s) most farmers kept a variety of animals; usually two to six cows, a flock of thirty or so sheep, a horse, fewer than twenty hens, some ducks and geese, and one or two pigs. The 1980s brought marked changes, however, as very few people now keep sheep, and the cows kept by small farmers are more for beef than domestically-used milk. There are noticeable exceptions, however, as some farmers have gone into the dairy business in an intensive manner. On one farm, for example, there are more than a hundred dairy cows and several thousand hens. As a result, several sizeable dairy farms have made the Valley one of the main suppliers of produce for western Newfoundland.

Until the 1970s, when fashions began to change rapidly, this area of Newfoundland was characterized by two main house types. The earliest type, of which only a few example remain (right, top), is a Cape Breton type, generally built before the end of the nineteenth century when a number of Cape Breton carpenters came to work and settle in the area. This style has largely disappeared as many of them were remodelled in the 1940s when a larger, two storey house became the preferred fashion. These larger houses (right, bottom), usually painted white or a pastel colour, have stood the test of time and are still admired for their fine craftsmanship.

Cape Breton style house: the MacArthur home in 1931, with Jenny MacArthur, her son Allan, and friend Angus MacLellan.

The MacArthur home remodelled in the new style of the 1940s (photo taken in 1971).

Usually the farms have a fairly large barn situated twenty or thirty yards from the house, the most common of which has a mansard roof (page 27, top), similar to those seen in Nova Scotia and common among the Pennsylvania Dutch. Often numerous other out-buildings are located near the houses (page 27, bottom) or attached to the barn: a hen house; a storage shed for tools or small farm implements; a shed formerly for keeping meat frozen in winter in the days before electricity, and today a convenient place for storing barrels of salted meat or fish. Occasionally there is a root cellar, though most people store their vegetables in the dug-out basements of their houses, which keep cool all year. Root cellars are common, however, in the area from Codroy to Cape Anguille, and this pattern seems to be more like that found in most other Newfoundland outports.

This description of the Codroy Valley is relevant only to the area within the actual physical valley structure, the area upon which this book focuses. As one leaves the section of Millville, travelling northwest toward the sea coast, a change of scenery emerges. The topography becomes more rugged, especially at Cape Anguille where the coast is very wild and windswept. The three coastal settlements of Woodville, Codroy, and Cape Anguille differ in more than scenery: the emphasis is no longer on agriculture but on fishing. Also the houses are situated much closer together than those in the Valley itself, and they are of a different type. They are much smaller houses, many with only one storey; brightly painted, they resemble the small, colourful houses of Newfoundland's Port au Port Peninsula. And lastly, it is interesting to note that the residents of these coastal settlements are of the Anglican faith while the other sections mentioned are almost all Roman Catholic.

Sawmills are another noticeable feature of the Valley, and several families own one of their own or share one with another family. The larger timbers are cut down and sawed into planks to be used for building. The outside strips of wood, cut off when the logs are squared before being cut into planks, are used for firewood. It is the job of young teenage boys in a family to cut these strips into one-foot lengths (usually called slabs) and stack them in sheds or in piles outside the home. Many people also cut wood specifically for fuel, but for this purpose most prefer the hard birch wood.

The conifers which grow in the Codroy Valley include larch, spruce, balsam fir and pine. There are also some hardwoods, principally maple, birch, and witch hazel. Winter wood cutting of coniferous timber supplements the income of many families while there is a lull in farming and fishing activities. The wood is cut in measured lengths and sold at a set price per cord, usually to

The photograph above shows a typical codroy Valley barn with mansard roof (1970). Below is Allan MacArthur's barn, showing additional storage sheds (1970).

Bowater's Pulp and Paper Company on the west coast of Newfoundland. Throughout the year, neatly stacked wood can be seen at the side of some of the backroads, all cut in a certain length and measured in cords, awaiting transportation by truck or train to the mill.

Fruit-bearing bushes and shrubs are plentiful in the Codroy Valley. Raspberry bushes grow in profusion along the roadsides in areas where trees have been cut down and no agricultural activities take place. There is an abundance of wild strawberries and, perhaps a little more difficult to find, gooseberries and choke cherries. On some marshy areas near the river, and in several swampy depressions within the backlands and mountains, one can find bakeapples (cloudberries) and marshberries. There is a good annual harvest of partridgeberries and blueberries from the barrens (the scrub area) on the edge of the Valley.

Although there are beautiful wild flowers all over Newfoundland, nowhere else do they seem so strikingly noticeable as in the Codroy Valley. Here they can be seen growing in roadside ditches, along the banks of rivers and streams, in fields, and among woodlands. There is an abundance of wild roses, sea-pinks, blue iris, harebell or Scotch bluebell, campion, bird's-foot-trefoil, speedwell, wild orchids, violets, celandine, pitcher plant, marsh marigold, and water lily, along with many other flowers and ferns. Alder bushes thrive in the damper areas near the rivers, where there are also several kinds of reeds and many mosses. In both the woodlands and meadows one can find several species of mushrooms.

Wildlife also abounds, and the early guidebooks noted that the Codroy Valley was an ideal place for the sportsman:

> The angler or tourist who arrives in Newfoundland by SS *Bruce* reaches some of the best salmon rivers in the Island almost at once. The railway from Port aux Basques (as will be seen by the small sketch maps) runs alongside the Little Codroy and Grand River Codroy for several miles.[1]

The Valley is still a popular place for tourists and sportsmen; and during the salmon and trout seasons there are many who visit to enjoy the sport of the fishing pools along the rivers. The local fishermen also fish in the coastal sea-waters for cod, herring, mackerel and lobsters. Several fishing boats can usually be seen tied up to the wharf at Codroy, and stacked nearby the pots used in the lobster fishery. The fish industry has been on the decline for many years, however, and today's fishery is nothing like the concern it once was.

For many years hunters have been known to visit the Codroy Valley to take advantage of the large numbers of caribou and, more recently, moose, which are found on the mountains further back from the settlements. In his book *Newfoundland and its Untrodden Ways* (London, 1907), J.G. Millais wrote a description and guide for hunters in Newfoundland. Written before the introduction of moose into Newfoundland, his section dealing with the Codroy Valley describes caribou hunting in the area. Local people have also hunted the Arctic hare and rabbits for their meat, and lynx for their fur. Although it is thought that the Arctic hare is rare in Newfoundland, there are reports that it is still seen in the Codroy Valley, though in considerably fewer numbers than in the days of the early settlers. There are also black bears, beaver, muskrat, weasels, squirrels, and other small animals. There are no reptiles in Newfoundland, and while the oldest inhabitants of the Codroy Valley mention that there are no amphibians either, today's youngsters enjoy chasing the frogs which have appeared in more recent years.

There is also a great variety of birds in the Valley. The local people hunt several species of game birds, including ruffed grouse, spruce grouse, black duck, and snipe. Along the many sandy beaches and shores can be seen great numbers of sea birds. In the summer, huge flocks of swallows and swifts congregate above the fields near the sandy mouths of the rivers, or can often be seen lined up in rows along the telegraph wires. One will also see robins, red-wing blackbirds, and other members of the thrush family, along with chickadees, juncos, and other small birds.

The lure of the Codroy Valley is perhaps strongest to all of those people whose people have lived in it and loved it for generations. Throughout the seasons young and old alike show endless enthusiasm for an early morning visit to the river, rod in hand; a trek into the woods to set or check rabbit snares; a family day out on the berry barrens; a weekend far into the bush at a hunting camp (Grandma will take care of the children); an outing with the children to dig clams from the white sand at low tide or to dive into the breakers as they come ashore. Often one or two figures can be seen to stand and gaze along the river or across the mountains, understating the praise they have repeated over the years: "It's some nice." They are well pleased with this corner of Newfoundland, the area once referred to as "God's Little Acre."

CHAPTER 2

The Garden of Newfoundland

Cha bhi toradh gun saothair.
[There will be no produce without labour.]
—*Gaelic Proverb*

Early Days

The Codroy Valley was already inhabited by Newfoundland's native people, the Beothuk Indians, when the first immigrants, Micmac Indians from Cape Breton, Nova Scotia, arrived. J.B. Jukes, Newfoundland's first geological surveyor, wrote what is probably the best description of early settlement in the area. Although he did not visit the Codroy Valley until 1839, his information is based on the oral traditions learned from his Micmac guide, Sulleon, and goes back to a much earlier period.

At the beginning of the last century [the eighteenth] a body of Micmac Indians, partly civilized and converted to the Roman Catholic faith, either came or were sent from Nova Scotia, and settled in the western part of Newfoundland. These were armed with guns and hunted the country, making great havoc amongst the game. A quarrel soon arose—perhaps on this account— between them and the Red Indians; and Sulleon gave me a confused account of a battle that took place between them at the north end of the Grand Pond about seventy years ago [c.1762]. In this the Red Indians [Beothuk] were defeated, as they were armed only with bows and arrows, and, according to Sulleon's statement, every man, woman, and child was put to death. [1]

Although the last Beothuk known to have lived in Newfoundland died at St. John's in 1829, Jukes reported that in 1839 his companions "were in continual dread of meeting the Red Indians" while travelling in the Codroy Valley and the mountains adjacent to it; they "evidently looked upon them as wild animals of a pernicious character."[2]

The first person to cross Newfoundland from east to west and publish an account of his travels was William Epps Cormack. Cormack journeyed across Newfoundland in 1822 accompanied by his guide and companion, a Micmac Indian named Sylvester. Cormack visited the Codroy Valley, where he observed that "at the Great and Little Codroy Rivers, towards the southern extremity of St. George's Bay, there are twelve or fourteen families, amounting to seventy or eighty souls, who catch annually four or five hundredweights of codfish, and about fifty barrels of salmon, and obtain a little fur."[3]

Cormack does not, however, make it clear what their nationality was. He may have been assuming that his reader would take it for granted that these "seventy or eighty souls" were not foreign (that is, not foreign to Cormack) and would assume, therefore, that they were probably English. He did, however, make this unusual comment:

> It may be that on the west coast of Newfoundland there is neither Scotchman, Irishman nor rat to be met with; nor, it is said, had any member of these European families taken up an abode west of Fortune Bay.[4]

Perhaps his odd phrasing suggests that there were English people there, but it is not clear exactly what he meant.

Nevertheless, Cormack was aware of the fact that the Micmac and French were living in the area and he described the situation he met in some detail:

> Owing to the shelter and anchorage for shipping at Codroy, ...and to its immediate proximity to the fine fishing grounds about Cape Ray, it is the central point of the French fisheries in summer. Many square-rigged vessels are here loaded with dried codfish for France; and hundreds of bateaux brought from France in the fishing-ships scatter hence in all directions over the fishing-grounds.... We crossed the gut, or entrance, between the sea and the extensive shallow entrance of this river in a boat of one of the residents. The entrance is barred with sand, and has only about six feet of water. There reside here five families with their servants, amounting to twenty-eight souls. They catch about forty barrels of salmon annually which, with herring and

a trifling cod-fishery, are their chief means of subsistence....
There were at this time ten Indian families encamped for the
winter on the banks of the Great Codroy River, about ten miles
from its mouth. The chief attraction for the Indian here is the
abundance of eels and trout.[5]

In 1835, an Anglican priest, Archdeacon Wix, made a
missionary journey round the coastal settlements of Newfoundland.
He sailed south from St. John's, then along the south coast to Port
aux Basques, and from there up to Codroy. Archdeacon Wix
mentions that he "saw a new vessel of seventy or eighty tons, which
some Basque people from the French Island of St. Peter's had,
contrary to treaty, built last winter on Codroy River."[6] This is one of
the earliest written references to boat building on the [Great] Codroy
River, although oral tradition reports much earlier instances.

Archdeacon Wix visited parts of the Codroy Valley. Stopping
first at the settlement at the mouth of the Little Codroy River where
he baptized several children, he then went on to the Great Codroy
River, stopped to hold services, and rowed across from the port of
Codroy to Codroy Island—a small island directly opposite the port
—in order to hold Sunday church services there. On this island
Archdeacon Wix saw much evidence of a thriving French fishing
industry. Even though it was Sunday, the French fishermen were
busy "brimming or caulking their boats and their crew were fishing
in the offing, as upon a weekday."[7]

The type of land and the climate of this part of Newfoundland
impressed the Archdeacon. He noted in his diary:

> From Cape Ray to this place [Codroy] the soil is so much
> improved that it is quite capable of being brought into
> cultivation; cattle are very numerous here already.[8] Between
> Cape Ray, indeed and the Bay of Islands, there is decidedly more
> land capable of being brought, with very little trouble, into
> cultivation, than in all the parts of Newfoundland with which
> several pretty extensive tours had made me previously
> acquainted. There is another advantage too, peculiar to this part
> of the coast; there is so little fog and dampness of atmosphere
> that fish may be laid out to dry here with much less risk than
> elsewhere of its becoming tainted.[9]

Jukes also made some interesting observations about the north
bank of the Great Codroy River. He had "heard reports of coal having
been seen by the Indians up the Codwy [sic] River"[10] and was
attempting to obtain more information on its exact location. He had
hoped to secure a guide from the Indians but they were reluctant to
impart any information and gave him several reasons for this:

I was also told that an Englishman named Gale, who lived on the south side of the river and who had the reputation of being very rich, had strictly charged the Indians to give no information. Those Indians who resided all the year round were sometimes dependent on the English settlers for food and dare not disobey them, and the latter were particularly churlish and incommunicative, especially old Gale.[11]

This mention of 'old Gale' is particularly interesting since oral tradition takes us back to the source of this report, some generations before the Gale mentioned by Jukes. Gale is one of the more common names in the Codroy Valley today and, so far as I know, none of the written accounts of the settlement of the Codroy Valley explain how or why the Gales settled there. The following account is from oral tradition and was given to me by one of the oldest Gales in the Valley, who heard it as a youth from older members of his family. Since he did not wish to be recorded on tape, the text here is from my field notebook, written down immediately after my visit with him in July 1970:

The first Gale was John Gale who came to the Valley about two hundred years ago. He came over to Newfoundland on a ship from England and came up the river on a long-boat. They found an ideal place on the Great Codroy River to build a schooner—probably it was about the place where Gillis' Cabins are now [this is a few hundred yards west of the Grand Codroy bridge; see map, page 4]. When the boat and crew were about to return home, John Gale asked permission to stay, and he asked them to leave what was left of the nails and other materials used in building the schooner. Well, he thought that much of the Codroy Valley!

He stayed in the Valley and became very friendly with the Indians who lived there at the time. After about three years in the Valley he took the boat that he had and went up around the coast, and he came back with a woman. No one knows where he got her—she wasn't an Indian woman. And he settled in the Valley with her. Now, no one knows if he married her or not—he probably just took her and lived with her! But they had a family, say, seven sons; and so it went on, and that's how there's so many Gales around. And some moved up and settled in Port au Port, some in Robinsons, and others in White Bay, but you don't hear of many around St. John's.

Now, there's thousands of dollars belonging to the Gales over in England, but they can't get the money out.

Mr. Gale also told me that the older men in the Valley who were familiar with the area of woods set back a good way from the Great

Codroy River knew of a graveyard which, they said, showed the earliest written record of the death of a Gale in the Codroy Valley. They refer to the gravestone of John Gale, which is dated 1815. They are of the opinion that he lived in the area for many years before his death, and this would date the arrival of the first Gale from the second half of the eighteenth century and would confirm Mr. Gale's estimation of about two hundred years ago. This is considerably earlier than indicated by any printed sources.

Another point of interest concerning the story of John Gale is the fact that his gravestone is a six-foot-long slab of stone. Because of its size, the local people do not believe it to be local stone. Today, only the sure-footed woodsmen know its exact whereabouts, for the area was "grown over years ago" and is now very difficult to reach.

The Arrival of the Scots

A few years after Jukes visited the Codroy Valley, the first Scottish immigrants arrived from Cape Breton, Nova Scotia. Rev. Michael Brosnan, a Roman Catholic priest and historian who based his writings on church records available to him in the 1930s,[12] described the arrival of the first Scots, some ninety years after it took place:

> The first arrivals seem to have come about 1844, but the immigration at the time was almost negligible. The lure was the stories that travelled to Nova Scotia of the wonderful fertility of the soil in many parts of the west coast of Newfoundland. It was also well known that it was easy to get a block of land which was gratis if one could hold it. Taxes were almost unknown.[13]

Brosnan states that by 1844 the Scottish families found in the Codroy Valley included "McNeills, McIsaacs, and McLeans." Others followed later and began to establish homesteads and clear land for cultivation.

Undoubtedly the main reason the Scottish immigrants came to Newfoundland when they did was their concern for land-ownership. In the first place, those who came from Scotland to 'America', as the old people called it, did so because they had been ousted from their crofts during the ruthless dispossession of the lands during the Highland Clearances, to make way for vast sheep farms. They had been forced to leave their native land and attempt to build for themselves a completely new life in a new country. North America offered an opportunity for such settlement, and many of these expatriate Scots settled in Nova Scotia.

Those who had arrived too late to take advantage of the earlier attractions that met the first migrants, however, were not at ease. It seems they had not been long in Nova Scotia when the question of land tenure became a problem once more. Several Scottish immigrants felt threatened that they might have to face the same situation they had already faced in Scotland at the time of their eviction and were, therefore, dissatisfied with the uncertainty of land tenure in Nova Scotia. Their sole concern was to own a piece of land they could cultivate. Consequently, according to Allan MacArthur, many families migrated within a decade or so to Newfoundland where they heard they would be free from heavy taxes and troublesome landowners.

The Scots were probably the first to settle in the Codroy Valley with the express purpose of owning land for farming. Up until their arrival those who were settling did so for the reason that most of Newfoundland was settled, namely for the codfishery.

Personal Memories of Emigration

In the early 1800s, Angus MacArthur, grandfather of Allan MacArthur, left the Isle of Canna in the Inner Hebrides of Scotland at the age of twenty-two to emigrate to Cape Breton, Nova Scotia. The exact date of Angus's emigration is not known, though Allan's information from family tradition dates the move around the 1820s. This is confirmed by census reports from the Isle of Canna, which are discussed in detail by the present laird of Canna, John Lorne Campbell, in his excellent book *Canna: The Story of a Hebridean Island* (Oxford, 1984). From his study on these reports, Dr. Campbell states:

> The 1821 Census shows a total population of 206 males and 230 females of both islands, total 436; and 73 inhabited houses. In the 1831 Census the figures are 124 males and 140 females, total 264; inhabited houses not recorded—a drop of 172. So there was certainly a substantial emigration between 1821 and 1831. Its exact circumstances are uncertain. According to a reply given by Robert Graham to Lord Teignmouth of the Committee on Emigration, the first thing done by Donald MacNeill I after purchasing the islands (of Canna and Sanday) had been to emigrate 200 of the inhabitants at his own expense.[14]

Of particular interest in Dr. Campbell's study is the "Rental of Canna Martinmas 1818" published in his book, for it shows a relatively large population of tenants bearing the name MacArthur (*Figure 1*). They were also included in the lists for 1820 and 1821. While the list of tenants remaining on the Island after the emigrants left would certainly have been adjusted accordingly, John Lorne Campbell comments on a later wave of emigration (the 1851 Clearance) that:

Figure 1

Rental of Canna Mart.ᵗ 1818

Donald MacNiel Esqr.		£373 10 –
Mrs Ann MacDonald	Sand Island	16 6 6
John Jameson	Do.	9 7 8
Niel MacIntosh	Do.	10 6 6
Hugh Jameson	Do.	9 2 4
Malcolm MacArthur	Do.	5 15 5
Finlay MacArthur	Do.	5 10 –
Widow Niel MacKinnon	Do.	5 1 10
Donald MacLean	Do.	5 10 –
Donald MacIntosh	Do.	5 10 –
John MacArthur Senr.	Do.	5 10 –
John MacIsaac	Do.	5 12 6
Allan MacArthur Junr.	Do.	5 12 6
Alex. MacArthur	Do.	5 12 6
John MacInnes	Do.	5 12 6
William Jameson Senr.	Do.	5 16 3
Niel Jameson	Do.	6 0 6
Mrs Alexr. MacDonald	Do.	14 6 0
William Jameson Junr.	Do.	6 2 –
Malcolm and Widow Campbell	Do.	9 16 –
Alexr. MacLeod and John MacArthur	Do.	9 16 –
Lachlan MacArthur	Do.	5 12 6
Angus MacLeod	Do.	– 16 8
Donᵈ Campbell	Do.	– 16 8
P. MacCarmic	Do.	– 16 8
Finlay MacCaskill	Do.	– 16 8
Malcolm MacArthur	Do.	– 16 8
Christian MacDonald	Do.	– 16 8
Lachlan Jameson	Do.	– 16 8
Edward Jameson	Do.	– 16 8
Lachlan MacIsaac	Do.	– 16 8
John MacCarmic	Do.	– 16 8
		£539 16 2

The rental list of the Isle of Canna in 1818, from the Estate Papers, courtesy of Dr. John Lorne Campbell of Canna.

It is unfortunate that no record of the names of the emigrants, nor of the immediate effects of the Clearance, survives but even ten years later the drastic reduction of population is obvious.[15]

With particular reference to Angus MacArthur's emigration, an enquiry to Dr. Campbell yielded further evidence:

Angus MacArthur is mentioned in a letter from Fr. Neil MacDonald, Barra, to his predecessor Fr. Angus MacDonald, who had left Barra towards the end of 1825 to become the Rector of the Scots College at Rome. Fr. Neil says he has paid an account of £12.8.8 from Angus MacArthur, from Canna.... Date of letter is 13/7/1828.[16]

The account was paid on Angus's behalf by the priest, but there is no mention of the date of the actual emigration. Presumably, however, Angus's departure for America was around this time. Bringing the history of the MacArthurs of Canna very much more up to date, John Lorne Campbell also added his own personal memory of them, a final note which will no doubt be of great interest to the many MacArthurs who now inhabit the Codroy Valley:

I knew the last of the MacArthurs here, Charles, very well. He was a lobster fisherman, a very decent, much respected, friendly person. Charlie died in November 1946... and was given a real wake in the old-fashioned style.[17]

According to Allan MacArthur's family tradition, his grandfather Angus was not the only member of that family to emigrate. He also had a younger sister who followed on a later boat, but she managed to return to Scotland soon afterwards, as she disliked Cape Breton. Allan considered that she was one of the few lucky ones:

A lot of people, when they arrived in Cape Breton, didn't like it but they had to stay as they couldn't go back. It was a wild place in those days; there was nothing like there is today.

In an interesting piece of oral tradition which still survived on Canna in the late 1940s, this same sentiment is echoed by an old man whose father had witnessed the emigrations of the mid-1800s. Thanks to the early recordings of the late Dr. Calum MacLean, one of the first collectors for the School of Scottish Studies in Edinburgh, who was then working for the Irish Folklore Commission, and to the scholarship of John Lorne Campbell, his account survives verbatim:

Chuir Clann 'ic Nìll uabhas dhaoine as an eilean. Cha chreid mi nach d'fhalbh trì fichead teaghlaichean as a'seo ri linn m'athair a bhith 'na dhuine òg. 'S e a' rud bu mhiosa dheth, chan fhaigheadh iad fuireach as a'rìoghachd seo fhéin. Bha iad air son

iad a dhol fairis co-dhiù. 'S ann a Chanada a chuireadh iad.
Chuala mi gun deach iad air bòrd an Tobar Mhoire. Bha iad a'
gealltainn dhaibh gum bitheadh iad gu math nuair a ruigeadh
iad a-null, ach 's ann a bha iad na bu mhiosa.

This was told on Canna by Angus MacDonald (b. 1863); it was
recorded and transcribed by Dr. Calum MacLean in 1949, and
translated by John Lorne Campbell:

> The MacNeills [who owned Canna at that time] put a terrible
> number of people out of the island. I believe that sixty families
> left when my father was a young man. The worst of it was that
> they couldn't remain in this country. Anyway, they wanted them
> to go overseas. They were sent to Canada. I heard that they
> embarked at Tobermory. They were promised that they would
> be well off when they had arrived over there, but in fact they
> were worse off.[18]

Having left Scotland to be rid of the hard regulations of landowners, it must have been disappointing to immigrants such as
Angus MacArthur to find a similar state of affairs in the new country.
Much of the land was already owned by people who had emigrated
many years earlier and had obtained land tenure on large areas. One
such landowner whom Allan MacArthur mentioned was Alexander
MacDonald, who came to Nova Scotia and settled in Antigonish
around 1784; and although Allan said he was not absolutely certain
of the accuracy of the date he gave, he did know that his grandfather
Angus MacArthur, like several other Scottish immigrants, lived and
worked on MacDonald's estate for some time after his arrival. From
oral tradition in Nova Scotia, Mary L. Fraser has obtained a parallel
account of a man who is probably one of this same MacDonald
family:

> Catholics began to come from the Highlands in 1785. They
> settled for the most part in Antigonish County and Cape Breton.
> Among the first arrivals was a great-hearted Highlander named
> MacDonald. He had built up a comfortable home before the full
> tide of immigration came in. His kindness to his fellow-
> countrymen on their arrival was proverbial. In one winter alone,
> no fewer than nine newly married couples among the
> immigrants were given big weddings at his house. One event of
> this kind would give much trouble and expense, for it meant
> entertaining the whole countryside with the best of everything
> that could be procured. Nine such events must have taxed even
> Highland hospitality.[19]

If indeed they were the same MacDonalds that Angus
MacArthur stayed with upon his arrival in the early 1800s, their

hospitality was no less than in previous days. Although Angus MacArthur did not settle there permanently, he nonetheless gained from his several years of living there. As his grandson said:

> He married my grandmother, Sarah MacDonald, you know, from [the family of] Alexander MacDonald that came out years before that.

This marriage was most likely in the mid-1830s, as the parish records of Searston, Codroy Valley state on the death certificate of one of their sons, Lewis MacArthur (father of Allan), that he was born in Cape Breton in 1840.

For several years the family of Angus and Sarah MacArthur lived in Cape Breton. They were, however, still no nearer to landownership, and Nova Scotia was in the midst of a lengthy pre-Confederation debate. The fact that any slim chance which might have existed for them to own land seemed to be threatened all the more by the prospect of Nova Scotia joining Confederation led to their decision to leave.[20]

Several Scots families had already made the decision to move to Newfoundland by this time. Allan MacArthur dates the MacArthur family move a few years after the migration of his mother's people, the MacIsaacs, who came to Newfoundland in 1854. The children and grandchildren of these families must have heard many times the account of why their peoples settled in Newfoundland:

> They started moving from Cape Breton on account of the hard rules and everything else—Cape Breton was a poor country too, but they were under Confederation rules and that was bad rules at that time; but the prices [this probably refers to the prices which were paid to farm workers for their cattle and produce] was so small and the land...well in Confederation rules you don't own the land, you don't own the house, you don't own the furniture, you owns nothing if you don't pay the taxes. Well, that's the rule. (But we got Confederation since 1949, but haven't got the *bad* rules of Confederation that Cape Breton used to have.) And they couldn't live under it.
>
> And those people, a lot of them left that settled from Scotland out to Cape Breton, and they lived there for a good many years— some of them not too long, probably ten, fifteen years—and they heard of Newfoundland, you see. Well, Newfoundland was a free country for anybody. And it was the Responsible Rules that we had. Well, the Responsible Government it didn't start the first starting of the people settling in Newfoundland, but it started years after. But...probably eighty years ago or a hundred years

ago you could come to Newfoundland and you could take up two, three, four hundred acres and there was no tax, there was nothing to pay; it was yours. And you could work on the farm and make your own living but you had to do everything.

Allan MacArthur's mother's maiden name was Jenny MacIsaac. Her father was a MacIsaac from Moidart and her mother a MacDonald from Glengarry. Although Allan could give little more information on their background in Scotland, the very mention of Moidart opens pages of detailed and significant history. In his book *Moidart; or Among the Clanranalds*, published in 1889, the Rev. Charles MacDonald, priest of Moidart, makes frequent mention of surnames which are now common in the Codroy Valley, and their part in the very significant Jacobite cause of the mid-eighteenth century:

> Most of those who followed the chief belonged to Moidart, Arisaig and South Morar, with a few from Eigg and Canna. Their total number did not exceed 300. There is a very interesting roll, unfortunately not complete, still preserved in the Clanranald family, giving the names of the Moidart men who had to 'rise' their places of residence and the armour, if any, which they could produce.[21]

Compiled in 1745, the list itself enumerates several MacDonalds and MacIsaacs (written MacIsaak), who were "thus summoned to draw the sword for Prince Charlie." After the ill-fated Battle of Culloden in 1746, those who survived the hardships were then faced with the dreadful aftermath which is documented in countless histories of Scotland. Eviction was the inevitable fate of many:

> From various causes, most of the families directly connected with this list have disappeared, some having emigrated to the colonies, others having left Moidart to settle in other districts and some having died out.[22]

Allan MacArthur's maternal grandparents emigrated to the New World in the mid-1840s when his mother, Jenny, was a very young child. Whether or not her account of their voyage across the Atlantic and their landing in Nova Scotia can be attributed to her actual memory as a tiny child is of little importance; her parents probably spoke of it often enough to refresh any memories she had of their emigration from Scotland and she, in turned, passed that information on to her own children:

> You can leave an t-Eilean Sgitheanach today and be home again tomorrow...but when my people came out, the MacIsaacs, it took them seven weeks on the boat from the time...bho'n deach iad air bàta ann an Tober Mhoire, agus...landed on the Gut o'

Canso. Nuair a' chunnaig mo Sheanair 's mo Sheanamhair an t-àit, nam biodh long a' dol a dh'Alba air ais cha tigeadh iad air tìr, ach bha 'm bàta dol do dh'Astrailia, agus...they would never have landed if the boat was going back to Scotland.

Since Gaelic was the language in which his mother narrated all her stories of their history and legend to her family, it was natural for Allan to revert to his mother tongue while re-telling the unforgettable experience of his own people. It bears repeating in the language of Allan's grandchildren:

> You can leave the Isle of Skye today and be home again tomorrow...but when my people came out, the MacIsaacs, it took them seven weeks on the boat from the time...from the time they went on the boat in Tobermory [Isle of Mull, Scotland, see map, page 6] and...landed on the Gut o' Canso [Cape Breton]. When my grandfather and grandmother saw the place, if the boat had been going back to Scotland, they wouldn't have landed; but the boat was going to Australia, and...they would have never had landed if the boat was going back to Scotland.

Allan MacArthur added that at one time he attempted to find out in Nova Scotia the name of the boat on which his forebears came, but he was unable to do so. This, he said, was because their boat had left Scotland after most of the immigrant boats, and the record of its sailing was not along with those of other immigrant lists of boats and their passengers who sailed from Scotland to Nova Scotia. Julie Morris, genealogical archivist of the Public Archives of Nova Scotia, affirms that: "Immigration records are virtually nonexistent until about 1867 when the federal government assumed responsibility for this field." In her booklet *Tracing Your Ancestors in Nova Scotia* she also adds that "Locating one's ancestors on a passenger list is a rare occurrence. Few lists have survived."[23]

The MacIsaac family settled in Inverness, Cape Breton, where they farmed along with other Scottish immigrants. For several years they made their home there, although they owned no land:

> They lived ten years down in Inverness, in Cape Breton, and then they got burned out, you know, lost everything they took from Scotland; then they moved to Newfoundland.

Although it was due to the hardships they met with in Cape Breton that the Scots left and migrated to Newfoundland, it was not hard work which deterred them. If they endured that in Cape Breton, they were required to do so all the more in Newfoundland. The most important thing was that they could at last own land. In order to be able to work the land they were required to clear large areas of timber, as the Codroy Valley was heavily wooded. The Scots settlers began to take their place in a land that had been hitherto settled for its fish, timber and fur. As one might expect, the demands on the newcomers were entirely different.

When the Scots came to the Codroy Valley in the 1850s it was, of course, nothing like it is today:

> After they came to Newfoundland...there was nothing ahead of them, only the forest and the river and the brooks. There were no roads, no post office, no stores, no church, no nothing like that—no mail, no mail at all; you wouldn't get mail probably for six months, and that would have to be brought in from St. George's with a dog team over the hills. And no guides, only old marks, you see, for to follow over the mountains. That's the way they lived.
>
> They thought it was a wild place to live in.

Having sailed up the Grand Codroy River, they came ashore at a place where there was not even a hut in which to shelter on the night they arrived. The MacIsaac family spent the first few nights under the shade of a large tree, until they had built their first dwelling:

> The first three days they spent there. And they had a lot of children, brothers and sisters, and they lived under a great big tree up there where Hughie McIsaac lives—where his father lived. And then they start building a camp, you know, kind of a shed for to shelter themselves. There were quite a lot of girls in the family, and boys too....Well, the boys and their father went out fishing, you see, for to get fish, and the old woman—the mother—and the girls they started building the camp. And according as they [the men] put up the logs, you see, the girls was in the woods picking up moss for to cork [sic, caulk] the logs between to make it warm; like, if you were building a ship or a boat you'd have to use oakum, and you'd have to use this marline rope and everything. And they were three days and then they built that house, and they lived in it.

While it would be difficult to find a tree in the Valley today that would be large enough to camp under, it is still obvious from the unusually wide floor planks in some of the very oldest houses that the first growth timbers must indeed have been huge.

Land clearing was heavy work. The new settlers cut down the big timber, and much of this wood they used in the building of their homes (*right*). A team of men then had to dig out the deep roots, using the powerful and ingenious lever device they called a 'stumper'. The roots were then burned to prepare the land for cultivation. The entire family shared in this work of preparing and planting the 'burnt

Aerial view of cleared lands along a section of the Grand Codroy River. The original MacArthur homestead (A) with adjacent farm buildings (B, C) overlook MacArthur Island, while Allan's son Frank and his family live next door (D). Frank's barn is E.

ground'. When describing the work done by the people of the Valley, Allan MacArthur had special regard for the diligence of the women, not only in the earliest days but also during his own childhood and early adulthood:

> When the babies would be about three weeks old, and she'd go out in the burnt ground, she'd make a little place for the baby alongside of a stump, and cover him up after feeding him, and she'd go on planting potatoes. You won't find women today who would do that.

It was an accepted fact that the women bore the greatest burden as far as the work was concerned.[24] For several generations after the first settlers arrived in the Valley this was the case. One of Allan MacArthur's sons, Frankie, spoke of how difficult it was for the early settlers in the Valley who, he said, "had it pretty tough.":

> ...and especially the women. It was the custom, as far as I know, especially with Scottish people here—Scottish men, you know—they expect an awful lot of their women. They expect them to do an awful lot of work. The men took it much easier than the women. I had an uncle, he told me that when a man got married, he said the first thing he got was a woman, then he got a hoe for her, then he had it all to himself. If you got a woman and a hoe, you made your living then.

In spite of the fact that living in Newfoundland presented many hardships to those who came, they were nevertheless happy with their new land (*below*). They were relieved to know that at least they

The field below Allan's house, looking over MacArthur Island and across the river to Millville.

would never be short of the things they had lacked in Cape Breton and Scotland before that:

> That's what they met in Newfoundland, but they were glad because they were clear of Confederation rules. We had a free country here; you could do what you liked. You could claim land, and catch fish, and catch game. The wild game was plenty all around, you know, like caribous and salmon and trout and eels and rabbits and the other kind we call the hare rabbits [Arctic hare]—they was twice as big as the normal ones.... You'd never starve because the woods was full of wild game.

Records of Church and State

Apart from the fact that every family which settled in the Codroy Valley had to work hard as a unit to establish the individual homesteads, there was another important aspect which cannot be ignored when describing the shaping of the newly-settled Codroy Valley: that is, the development of the network of communities that made up the Codroy Valley, as opposed to the numerous family or ethnic units within the Valley.

Family traditions, such as those of the Scottish Gaels or the French, tend to be best preserved by the actual families involved. There were, however, a few incomers to the Valley who were able to look at the early settlers from a wider angle, thus taking in a larger, overall picture of the interaction between the various groups living there. These particular incomers also differed from the other immigrants in that their purpose of coming was not to obtain land to set up a family homestead but to provide certain necessities to the lives of those who did. Most notable among these were the Roman Catholic priests, and fortunately a few of their interesting observations have been preserved in writing.

Today the people of the Codroy Valley are very much aware of the fact that the Roman Catholic Church has been the greatest driving force behind most of the development of their area. The influence of the Church was not upon those settled in the Valley, or where or when. It was rather in working for better living conditions for all the settlers, in trying to obtain for the residents what they considered to be essential to the lives of the people: namely, someone to minister to their spiritual needs, a means of educating the children, and a programme of road construction to alleviate some of the problems of isolation.

The work of the Roman Catholic Church was harassed by several difficulties. According to Monsignor Thomas Sears, the "greatest draw-back being the want of roads or other means of communication" in his large parish which included the Codroy Valley:

> To describe the annoyance and inconvenience arising from this defect...just imagine three thousand souls dispersed over some eight or nine hundred miles of sea-coast (it will take that distance when we compute the various indentations of our bays over which the messenger of the Gospel must pass). It is easy to conceive what obstructions this isolation casts in the way of administering to spiritual wants, and the hardships of the missionary in undertaking such journeys; journeys which for him will never end, with no road but the trackless forest, the sea-beaten land-wash, or the still more unpleasant alternative of going either in an open boat or a cranky fishing skiff, along this whole coast.[25]

Soon after his arrival on the west coast of Newfoundland in 1850, Father Alexis Belanger realized that he was faced with a language problem in the Codroy Valley area. Father Belanger wrote his records in his native French and, being bilingual, was able to administer to the needs of all those who spoke English and French. This was not sufficient, however, to meet the needs of all the people in his district:

> The settlers who had come in from Inverness, Cape Breton, almost without exception used the Gaelic language as the language of the home. Though many of them had a passing knowledge of English, they had not sufficient command of it to make their confessions with facility and to their own satisfaction.[26]

Father Belanger attempted to secure a "yearly visit from a priest versed in the silver speech of the Gael, the mother tongue of so many of his people." He was successful in doing this in the years 1866, 1867 and 1868, when the Gaelic-speaking priests Fathers Shaw, Chisholm and Fraser visited the Valley.[27]

Most memorable of the early priests was Father (later Monsignor) Thomas Sears who in 1868 became the first resident priest of the Parish of St. George's. He remained there until his death in 1885. Thomas Sears, who was born in County Kerry, Ireland in 1824, emigrated to America with his parents at the age of eight. They settled in Nova Scotia where this Irish Gael gained knowledge of the Scottish Gaelic of Cape Breton.

A number of weeks after his arrival in Newfoundland, Father Sears wrote down his impressions of the Codroy Valley in a letter to the Bishop of St. John's, the Right Reverend J.T. Mullock, D.D.

Written twenty-four years after the arrival of the first Scots, it seems to be the earliest detailed description of the Codroy Valley, along with his views on its development and potential:

This seems to me to be a very important portion of the grand Island of Newfoundland. This Bay, with its tributary rivers as well as several other localities along this coast, affords better inducement—at least in my estimation—than the United States to the fishermen of St. John's and other places who are emigrating. In this Bay alone there are now as many vessels at anchor as will require, it is estimated, 70,000 barrels of herring to load them; still, although herring did not strike in till after the 22nd of this month [November 1868] such is the quantity taken the last five or six days, that they are all in hope of getting fair cargoes. They tell me that the Codfish is quite plentiful in the Bay if they could attend to it.

There is another advantage, I perceive, that this Bay enjoys and that is the fertility of the soil, and the magnificent forests which line the bays and rivers especially. It seems that there is no land superior to this for the cultivation of green crops and hay; potatoes grow as well as in any part of North America; oats and barley, of course, will do as well; cabbage can be produced in abundance.

There have been two sawmills erected here lately. One will be in operation in a few days; it is constructed on the most improved principle and will drive as many saws as will saw the largest pine log in a pass. The pine is of enormous size, as large as any I ever saw in Nova Scotia or New Brunswick, and farmers who came here from Prince Edward Island say that the land is far superior here in point of fertility to that of the Island.

Add to this the fact of this Bay having—as it is calculated—always been the winter resort of all the Labrador herring which swarm along the coast, and which can be taken in the dead of winter as well as in summer, when people are idle in all the other harbours of our fishing coast. I am very much mistaken then if this Bay does not hold out an inducement to the poor fishermen who have to leave other parts of this Island. [It is] superior to the most glittering prospects held out by Gloucester or any other fishing districts in the United States, with this great difference, that while in the latter places the fishermen are exposed to such and so many dangers that numbers of valuable lives are yearly lost, in this River the fisherman is as safe while catching his fish as he is while sitting in his house in the bosom of his family.[28]

In the book which he later wrote, Sears noted that "the inhabitants of the Codroy Valley are principally of Highland Scotch origin with a sprinkling of Acadians and a few Irish."[29] The Irish people settled mainly on the north bank of the Grand Codroy River, in the place now known as O'Regan's. The English, Scottish and French settlers also seem to have settled in ethnic groups, each one choosing an area that would not interfere with the Micmacs, who had already settled on Indian Hill. According to Jukes, there was harmony among the different nationalities in the Valley:

> They all of all nations seem to live comfortably and
> peaceably together; and the only want I heard expressed was a
> wish for the establishment of schools in St. George's Bay.[30]

During his sixteen years in the large parish of St. George's, Monsignor Sears travelled to all areas of settlement along the eighty-mile stretch of land, although he located the priest's residence at the southernmost part, in the Codroy Valley. He spent his time in untiring activity in an effort to stir the government, church and people of Newfoundland into an awareness of the needs of the region which had, up until this time, been neglected.

By the time Monsignor Sears had arrived, the Scottish population had increased to a number considerably more than the few immigrants who came in 1844. Of them, he wrote:

> There is not a race that ever were blessed with a knowledge
> of God's Church more steadfast than the Catholic Highlanders.
> There are about sixty families of this class.[31]

Monsignor Sears left in his records and letters substantial evidence of what his parish was like and of his aspirations to better the living conditions there; fortunately, Brosnan had access to his writings. Sears was very much aware of the natural resources and advantages of the Codroy Valley, but was equally aware of the needs:

> It would be most desirable that the Government of St. John's
> should do something towards establishing some sort of civil
> authority, and something for the cause of education on this
> coast. Another great want is felt here—there are no roads, not
> even pathways.[32]

As far as obtaining favourable consideration from the Newfoundland government was concerned, the Codroy Valley was in these days in a politically uncomfortable position. It was part of that controversial territory known as the French Shore, so-called because the French held the fishing rights on this coast from 1713 to 1904. The French Shore at that time extended from Cape St. John to the Strait of Belle Isle. Although the residents were taxed like other Newfoundlanders, they had no representatives in the House of Assembly. Consequently, they did not receive the same consideration for improvement and development as did other areas of Newfoundland. In 1881, Sir Frederick Carter, KCMG, Chief Justice of Newfoundland, announced in his speech from the throne that the government was authorized to make grants of land on the French Shore and that the residents were to elect two representatives to the House.[33]

It took Monsignor Sears thirteen years of working in the Valley before his plans for road-building began to come to fruition. When the state of taxation without representation ceased to exist along the French Shore, several petitions for road-building on the west coast were put forward on behalf of the people by their representatives in the House of Assembly, many of which are recorded in the *Journals*. This resulted in their receiving government assistance to allow them to commence work on the roads which Monsignor Sears had planned. His two main aims were to set up lines of communication between the Codroy Valley and Port aux Basques, Corner Brook, and St. John's, and to link the outlying settlements within the Valley itself.

In a report on "Survey of Lands in the Codroy Valley," 1883, by James P. Howley, the author stated that he was impressed by the hard work of the people of the Codroy Valley:

> My experience of the past season convinces me more than ever that the proper class of settlers of our wild lands, and the only persons who will succeed in turning them to account, are those whose position in life of necessity compels them to labour hard with the sweat of their brows, till by dint of the most persevering toil, they succeed in laying the foundation of comforts and prosperity; if not for themselves at least for their posterity. Of such a class as this the hardy Cape Breton Highlander and Acadian French, who for the most part occupy the lands of the Codroys, are a splendid example.[34]

From all accounts, it is evident that Monsignor Sears possessed remarkable ability in organizing and encouraging the local people to participate in the projects which were essential to the improvement of the area. Brosnan gave this account:

> [Monsignor Sears] taught them and insisted on their learning the lesson that they should also help themselves and each other. His was to educate the people, not to nurse them.
>
> Another means by which he gained two good ends at the one time was by asking for free labour, not alone for the erection of churches and schools and presbyteries, but even for public works such as road-building. His activities in this sphere were successful and won for himself, his people and the fruits of their activities, this notable encomium on the floor of the House of Assembly.

We have marked instances of superiority of the road labour in that part of the country [Codroy Valley] as compared with other portions. I have no hesitation in saying that the superiority and management is due entirely to the controlling genius of the one who has proved himself the guardian angel, as it were, of that part of the country since he has gone there. I refer to Monsignor Sears. So heartily are the people there alive to the development of their large agriculture resources that they have come forward manfully and subjected themselves to statute labour in order to open up new roads and keep the others in repair. This is a condition of affairs not realized in any other district of the Colony.[35]

Besides the giving of free labour, there was also the practice of 'fishing for the church' which was organized by Monsignor Sears and involved the donation of the proceeds of an entire day's fishing to the credit of the priest, thereby allowing the accumulation of funds for the building of a church. This same idea was applied to those who were involved in winter wood-cutting, and was continued until there was enough money to commence building. They did not operate on the loan system which is common today.

During his twenty-seven years as resident parish priest, Monsignor Thomas Sears is remembered for his remarkable diligence. Regrettably, not all his parish records survived the 1930 fire, but among those that did is this entry of baptism:

Allan MacArthur, born 12 May 1884, son of Lewis MacArthur and Jeannie (nee MacIsaac), baptised by Thomas Sears on July 6, 1884.

When Monsignor Sears died in 1885 there were schools and churches throughout the Diocese of St. George's, there was a mail service to the area, the telegraph system extended from east to west, and "every important part of the fertile valley, 'the Garden of Newfoundland', was penetrated with roads."[36] By the year 1897 the railway line from St. John's to Port aux Basques, which passes through the Codroy Valley, was completed.

In the years that followed Monsignor Sears' death, several of the priests were very influential in the Valley. Among them was Monsignor Andrew Sears, a cousin of the first Monsignor Sears, who served in the Codroy Valley from the early 1900s until his death in 1944. Among the older inhabitants he is still a well-remembered figure.

Monsignor Andrew Sears was responsible for dividing the Parish of St. Anne's into 'sections' bearing the names of the present villages. He encouraged the residents of each one to take an interest in the affairs of their own section. During his term in the parish, a school was built in each section, and Monsignor Sears also planned churches for the same. The latter plan was not put into effect. Instead, church services were centralized at two Roman Catholic churches, one at Searston at the mouth of the Grand Codroy River, and the other at St. Andrews at the mouth of the Little Codroy River. Both were magnificent landmarks and a testimony to fine craftsmanship.

Changed Days

With the march of time came changes not only for the Codroy Valley but for all of Newfoundland. By the late 1960s there was a definite educational trend toward centralization of schools. Where the Valley was concerned, just as in days gone by, the issue came under the influence of the Roman Catholic Church. The central site was chosen at what seemed to be an ideal location, on the south side of the Grand Codroy River, close to the bridge. Father R. White, parish priest at the time, devoted much time and energy to fund-raising and organization of the successful establishment of Belanger High School. The new school, named after the first resident priest, was created to meet the needs of all children in the Valley; primary, elementary and high school. A system of transport, the now familiar yellow school bus, was set up to bring them all to this central school.

The opening of Belanger High School:
Allan MacArthur salutes the occasion with a bagpipe march.

Opening day was a special occasion, well-remembered for its sense of achievement and happiness. Children who were too young to know him personally still show photographs and recall the grand old man of more than eighty who played his bagpipes to open their school—Allan MacArthur (*page 51*). It was a day of community spirit and unity, its success largely attributed to Father White who unfortunately was moved to a new parish not long afterwards.

Progress in the Codroy Valley has had a long and energetic history. What must have seemed like a mammoth road-making task in the days of Monsignor Thomas Sears has now been achieved beyond his exhortations. The final link with the rest of the province was completed when the section of the Trans Canada Highway, from Port aux Basques to the Codroy Valley, was paved in 1966. In 1970 work began on paving the secondary roads within the Valley, and it still goes on.

Not all changes that have appeared in the name of progress, however, have met with the same warm welcome as did the school and the roads. Sadly, the majestic church at Searston, the centre of worship for all the settlements of the Grand Codroy River and which, during research for this book, was still the hub of the communities, is no longer there. In spite of the noticeable anguish of many residents young and old alike, the newer regime within the Church decided to build a modern one beside Belanger High School. Next to the church and school was also built a new priest's residence; a modern bungalow replacing the serene and elegant priest's house which had, even in the early 1970s when I visited it, a delightful air of Victoriana. Despite local protests it too was demolished in the mid-1970s, while many residents watched helplessly. Now in the 1980s, only a few briar rose bushes remain on the site that once upheld the magnificent Searston church. It had not only borne the name of the man who was the driving force behind the community but also the outstanding craftsmanship, today quite unmatched, had been a memorial to the Codroy Valley settlers who built it.

The work involved in this new centralization project was not without its setbacks. In January, 1972 the entire Valley was shocked to learn that their famous concrete bridge (*right*), the focal point of this entire scheme, collapsed like a pack of cards during a sudden thaw in the river. Miraculously, nobody was injured, but it came as no surprise to hear the name of Monsignor Sears murmured by several residents who wondered at the course of events. Civil engineers were immediately brought into the Valley to survey the damage and reconstruct a new link across to the north side of the river. Ironically, they chose to launch a Bailey Bridge across the mouth of the Grand Codroy, the Gut as locals call it—the very part of the river overlooked by the old Searston church.

Today a new bridge spans the river, and modern split-level houses are gradually replacing many of the fine old homes. The new houses may well be the 'last word' in luxury, with glossy magazine appeal, but the old style has a serene sense of history reflecting a stalwart past.

Despite the many changes the Valley has undergone, today's visitor still encounters people who are conscious of their ethnic background, be it Scottish, English, Irish, French, or a combination of these nationalities. The Micmac Indians no longer inhabit the Valley, as the last of them died from tuberculosis or left for Cape Breton in the 1930s during Newfoundland's economic depression. There are, however, a few people who through intermarriage have Micmac ancestry.

All the inhabitants of the Valley are now English speaking, though there are several people who also speak Gaelic or French. Unfortunately, however, neither of these languages has been passed on to the youngest generation in the Valley today. One reason given for this is that intermarriage between different ethnic groups has been more common during the past thirty years than it was in the preceding years.

There still remain, however, strong ethnic traditions about the people of the Codroy Valley which are especially noticeable among the older inhabitants. The culture of the Scottish Gaels is only part

The old bridge across the Grand Codroy River, once known as the "longest concrete bridge in Newfoundland," is no longer there.

of what makes up the complete picture of the Codroy Valley, and there is inevitably much overlapping across ethnic backgrounds. Nevertheless, there is still much that has always been peculiar to the Scottish settlers and it is these traditions, along with several more that cut across the other ethnic groups, which are represented here.

CHAPTER 3

Céilidh air Ailein MacArtair:
A Visit with Allan MacArthur

> I could keep you up all night telling you stories
> and singing you songs!
> *Allan MacArthur, 1970*

To the old Gaelic speaking people in Scotland and the New World, the word *céilidh* simply meant "a visit." The word was applied not only to the common, informal situation when a neighbour called in to see the people next door, however briefly, but also to the formally arranged social gathering of family and friends invited to a particular house to enjoy an evening together. Many books discuss the ceilidh as a source of entertainment, usually music and dancing, as if that were its only function. In fact, today the word has taken on a new usage, generally meaning a concert to the Scottish, a dance to the Irish, or occasionally elements of both. The word has been misused by English-speaking people to such an extent that even most Gaelic speakers accept it as the use of the Anglicized plural 'ceilidhs' (for *céilidhean*) clearly attests.

In the words of Allan MacArthur, a ceilidh meant "if you were going visiting friends, like céilidh air [Ian] MacLeoid" (like a visit with [Ian] MacLeod). The céilidh was, in fact, largely responsible for keeping all the Scottish Gaelic oral traditions alive, both in Scotland and in the parts of America settled by Gaelic speakers.

In every Gaelic community there were certain houses which were well-known to all and generally referred to as *taigh céilidh*, a céilidh house. There, in the home of a respected, well-recognized

55

tradition-bearer who, in advancing years, took the place once held by one or other of his forebears, the neighbours would gather on the long winter evenings. Daylight long-since faded and the outdoor tasks of the day over, the neighbours would meet at a chosen *taigh ceilidh*, "perhaps this one tonight, and that one tomorrow night."

Seated around the kitchen stove by the light of an oil lamp, the evening's activities would proceed. The women were usually carding, spinning, knitting, or mending. While the men in the Codroy Valley sometimes helped with the carding—and from time to time were occupied by such indoor winter crafts as cobbling, moccasin making, or ice-skate making—in general, their evenings tended to be much more leisurely than those of the women, whose hands were endlessly busy throughout the duration of each ceilidh.

On these long winter's evenings those gathered would listen to the stories and songs of their own people. To those who took part, it was no surprise that some of their traditions survived several centuries, for this was undoubtedly the surest way of preserving them. For those whose life demanded unending hard work, these stories and songs provided the only form of entertainment, while at the same time they made such tasks as carding or mending less monotonous:

> Our people could view the coming winter with few or no forebodings of straitened circumstances or pressure of economic conditions, and their minds were free to dwell on things imaginative and ideal—things pertaining to a higher plane than the mere vegetating bread-earning machine can aspire. To this then must be ascribed the idealism, the romance, the chivalry, and the poetry of the Scottish Highlands. In circumstances such as these only could such an institution as the ceilidh become possible: and the ceilidh in the Scottish Highlands became a school in which not only was information acquired and were ideas formed, but in which character and conduct were moulded.[1]

This description from Scotland fits equally well in the Codroy Valley where the Gaelic speaking Scots carried on the traditions of the ceilidh for generations. The MacArthur house was only one of several well-visited ceilidh houses in the days when such was the way of life.

Comparing what Allan MacArthur considered to be a "good memory" to what most people today regard as the same, it might seem that he belonged to another era. Today, nobody is required to amass facts that can be found in easily available reference books. In the early days of places like the Codroy Valley such books were completely unavailable, and printed material of any kind was scarce. There were, however, people who acted in place of these things; they were living reference sources of historical facts and legends. This pattern compares closely with the bardic pattern found in Scotland. The bardic tradition was partly oral, partly literary, and the bards themselves were required to have phenomenal memories. D.S. Thomson cites instances in Scotland where songs have survived through three hundred years of oral transmission with no assistance of printed texts.[2]

Whether in Scotland or in Scottish settlements across the Atlantic, the bearers of this strongly oral tradition displayed remarkable qualities:

> In general, they were men of high intelligence and keen minds, passionately interested in tales, widely educated in the oral learning of the Gaelic race.[3]

Allan MacArthur described his own memory as "the schooling he got from God." He himself could fit into the rare group of people described by Kenneth Jackson when he wrote of Scottish storytellers:

> Their minds were not cluttered with all the miscellaneous rubbish with which we burden ours, and they were not in the habit of pigeon-holing knowledge in the form of written notes and forgetting it till it is wanted again, as we are.[4]

In his youth, Allan MacArthur grew up to listen to people of remarkable memory. If one was to be considered a "good storyteller" then it would be expected that he would have that kind of mind which Kenneth Jackson described. By today's standards, perhaps, it seems that demands were high but that was their tradition—to be good, you had to have an excellent and well-trained memory. With this kind of background, one can see why Allan MacArthur felt let down at times when, through lack of opportunities to practice, his memory failed him and did not meet his own standards.

According to Allan, the one who stood out for him as a memorable bearer of his Scottish traditions was his own mother, Jenny MacArthur. Born in Scotland she was, from all accounts, like her mother before her, a very talented woman. She had a phenomenal memory and was thoroughly versed in her culture: the singer of songs, the narrator of history, tale, and legend, the skilful craftswoman. This outstanding tradition-bearer was to her generation what her son Allan was to his.

As he listened throughout childhood and adolescence to the conversations, songs and stories of his parents' and grandparents' generations, Allan became a link in the chain which carried those traditions to the next generation. No radio or television distracted him or cluttered his childhood mind as he sat in the company of adults, acting like the other children of his generation, silent throughout the duration of any visit. By the time he reached adolescence, he had heard the old people telling and retelling stories of their migration from Scotland to America and of the pioneer days in the Valley.

Allan MacArthur listened to a great diversity of topics discussed at the ceilidhs. He heard descriptions of the Highlands and Islands of Scotland, its scenery and (by Newfoundland standards) 'soft' climate; historical dates of important events in the lives of the Scottish people which he committed to memory; interpretations of ideas about the Battle of Culloden, the Highland Clearances, and Bonnie Prince Charlie; and stories of such characters as Dr. Samuel Johnson, the famous traveller, and George Buchanan, tutor to King James VI. And Allan listened to a fund of general information on life in the New Country also, where skills of survival were essential. As the area had no local doctor for over a century, they repeated the tested and tried cures or treatments for medical problems. The information was accessible to all at the ceilidh house: how to soothe a sore throat with goose grease on flannel, or relieve the common cough with cherry bark syrup; how to ease the pain of pleurisy with a mustard plaster; how to aid healing of small cuts with spiders' webs, or to staunch the bleeding of more serious ones by immersing the wound in the flour barrel; where to find in the Valley the help of a healer with special powers, such as the seventh son who could cure 'King's evil'; or one who could cure backache.

The ceilidh was the place where they affirmed their knowledge not just of how to stay alive in this new country, but of how to make a living. There they discussed the various duties required in the general care of their livestock and farmland, or learned to forecast the weather. There they listened to whatever the older people cared to talk about when they were together. Along with all of this, they also heard songs, stories, and instrumental music, and watched the best step-dancers of the day.

Despite the seemingly strict code of behaviour demanded from children, parents and grandparents liked to know nevertheless that the young people were there, interested in the traditions of their culture and learning about it as they themselves had done generations before. When he reached his old age, however, Allan MacArthur found that times had changed. Although his own children had all spoken Gaelic as their first language, by 1970 they used it only on rare occasions, such as at a ceilidh or party when they might bring up a childhood memory, or recall an adolescent prank, or engage in quick-witted amusement. In spite of the fact that they were familiar with their father's repertoire of Gaelic songs and could name the titles when requesting he sing one, they themselves knew only a few complete songs in Gaelic; most often their knowledge was restricted to the choruses or repetition line. By the time his grandchildren were growing up (with the exception of the family of his eldest son, Lewis, who married a Gaelic-speaker) English was the language of their homes. Though all the family were proud of the grand old man, with his keen mind and outstanding ability as a tradition-bearer, they could not alter the rapid changes time brought.

It was, then, in the context of the many dozens of ceilidhs with the MacArthur family that I was given a wealth of material from the traditions of the Codroy Valley as they knew them. Just as Allan and Mary in their youth heard all their traditions filtered through their elders, so they also selected the aspects which were most important to them, and which they wished to pass down to the following generation. Rather than having the choice of material determined by me or any other folklorist then, Allan MacArthur was the key figure in controlling what went on.

The many dozens of ceilidhs I shared with the MacArthurs were very much the old style ceilidh as opposed to the visiting which is common today, where guests and hosts will be quite likely to spend the evening following a favourite television serial. And in that old style I was a participant at the ceilidh, sometimes singing a song or two, and other times providing the comparisons which Allan wished to make between the way of life in the Valley and the Scottish Highlands. The reader will have already gathered that this book is totally the product of a participant-observer—my pleasures included holding hanks of wool for winding; mending the odd sock; 'topping and tailing' berries for jam; sharing a magazine or newspaper article, perhaps from that week or from a cutting that Allan had kept over the years; reminiscing over old photographs and looking at his picture postcard collection through an old-fashioned stereoscope he had bought in Boston in the early 1900s; or simply resting near the warmth of the kitchen stove: "Put your feet up on the daybed, now. I'm after getting tired myself."

Allan did not have a large collection of books, but he greatly treasured what few he had. One of his most valued was a copy of *Sàr-Obair nam Bard Gaelach: The Beauties of Gaelic Poetry and Lives of the Highland Bards* [5] which his friend Angus MacLennan had given him before his death many years previously. It was well-worn, and had no cover, but Allan kept it well out of reach of anyone who might not give it the care and respect it deserved. Though Allan could not read the Gaelic texts in this anthology, he could recognize the songs which were familiar to him. Of great interest to him were the sections in English, namely the general introduction to the book and the concise biographies of all the bards. One of the earlier Gaelic books to be printed in Nova Scotia, this particular book was apparently very popular among the Highland Scots there who welcomed and valued it in their Gaelic-speaking families.[6] In Scotland, too, *Sar Obair* was tremendously popular and acknowledged as stabilizing song texts in print. Presumably Angus MacLennan originally got Allan's copy on a visit to Cape Breton, as there has always been considerable communication between people in the Valley and their compatriots in Cape Breton.

Allan MacArthur had the same interest in print that was typical of many Highland Scots of his generation, although he did not have the same access to books. This interest is understandable, however, considering the fact that the Scottish education system of the nineteenth century was one which strongly emphasized literacy in all children while Newfoundland, being a relatively new country, did not have the same urgency toward literacy until much later. It was, nevertheless, very noticeable to me that Allan and Mary MacArthur both displayed strong literary traits which markedly contrasted with the frequent illiteracy found among much younger Newfoundlanders in other parts of the province. This particular feature undoubtedly came from the lack of opportunity rather than any lack of ability. The respect that Allan had for any printed material which entered his house must have been quite unmatched, for there were many Saturdays when I watched him go through the same procedure upon the arrival of his weekly newspaper. It was the weekend edition of the *Western Star* from Corner Brook, which consisted of two or three sections and a "Weekend Magazine." As soon as it arrived he would take a long darning needle with some homespun grey woollen yarn and make a few large bookbinder's stitches down through the centre fold of the pages to secure them so that the paper would withstand a week's wear. Only after he had done this would he sit down and enjoy reading it. Needless to say, no other member of the family would read it either, until it had been stitched in this way. By the time the next weekend's paper arrived, he would have read the previous one from cover to cover.

Although unable to read Gaelic, Allan had a few books and Cape Breton newspaper clippings which contained Gaelic songs. If he studied the words long enough he would recognize whether or not he knew a certain song, but he could not learn any new songs by this method, nor could he write down the Gaelic words of the songs he had learned orally, as the spelling and pronunciation system in Gaelic is completely different from that in English.

I recall one afternoon when my mother was with me, and Allan brought his old copy of *Sàr-Obair nam Bard Gaelach* to her to show her a certain song. He pointed out that there were verses printed which he did not know and asked her if she would read them to him and teach him the words. During the session the two of them sat down and read and repeated the words until Allan knew them to his own satisfaction. Even at the age of eighty-six he said that there was always something new he wanted to learn, and I got the impression that literacy in the Gaelic language was high on his list.

It was only in the early 1960s that Gaelic ceased to be the language of the MacArthur home. Allan said that up until that time they spoke nothing else except when they had company who could not understand Gaelic; then they would speak in English. It was obvious that Allan regretted their change of language, a regret he showed when he quoted the proverb:

Mun dubhairt e: 'Bho'n chaill mi a'Ghaidhlig na b'fhearr cha d'fhuair mi.'

As he said: 'Since I've lost the Gaelic language nothing better have I found.'

A ceilidh with the MacArthurs did not necessarily mean a recording session. Circumstances, or sometimes Allan himself, dictated that. The one question which always hovered in my mind throughout my first month in the Valley was how often could I visit without imposing on the family who had told me to "come any time." I remained self-restricted to two or (at most) three visits a week until one day I met one of their young granddaughters, Karen, who had been "up visiting Grandma and Grandpa MacArthur." Naturally I enquired of them, and her reply answered the question once and for all: "Know something? Grandpa was sitting on that bench out by the front door, looking through his binoculars to see if he'd see your car coming over our side of the river to visit him. Grandma says he's always looking out...." From then on a ceilidh with the MacArthurs was an almost daily event, as natural as if it had always been so. Whenever I went into the house Allan would usually be found reading, talking, or working at some small task, sitting in 'his own chair'—a wooden armchair that a friend had made for his birthday many years earlier—at the head of the big kitchen table. If the weather was particularly hot, he would move to the sitting-room, away from the oil and wood stove that burned daily, regardless of the season. Occasionally, I would find him taking a walk in his garden of fruit bushes or around the barn or woodpile. Sometimes he simply sat outside his house on a wooden bench in the shade, looking over MacArthur Island where his cattle sometimes grazed, to the north bank of the river and all around him, taking in the comings and goings of the Valley.

Although in his late eighties, the Allan MacArthur I knew was extremely mentally alert. He was interested in all that went on around him and loved to have someone to talk with him about history, politics, current affairs, music or simply the weather. He had a way of turning even a conversation about the weather into a topic of historical interest; like the time he compared today's climate to that of his youth when, he said, they could start ploughing in April as the winters then, though much colder, ended sooner, and the summers were hotter and longer. Today, he added, they have to wait till June to plough. He philosophized on that occasion that the earthquake of November 18, 1929 had an effect on the climate. It was never the same after, he said, for even the 'eel grass' that used to grow in the river disappeared completely. That Allan should still remember the actual date was as much a fascination to his listener as the disappearance of the eel grass.

For all the days we recorded there were many, many more when I simply left the machine in the car, and made no mention of it. Perhaps the summer's day was too hot or humid, and a quiet rest in the shade seemed best for all. There were times, too, when the old gentleman seemed tired or unwell; and on these days he would sit back or lie down and would sometimes ask me to tell him stories about Scotland, about my home there, and the domestic and agricultural practices. At times, he would ask me to sing Gaelic songs which I had learned from my mother; other times he lay down on the kitchen daybed while I spent time with Mrs. MacArthur. The luxury of being able to do this was one of the greatest advantages of living in the community for a number of months at a time. I never had the feeling that any of these quiet days were wasted—it was all part of getting to know the MacArthurs. On the rare occasion when I didn't manage a visit I found myself on the next day answering Allan's enquiring statement, "We didn't see you yesterday?" Far from creating any feeling of restriction on my days, it was all the more reassuring of the importance of our ceilidh, no matter how informal.

Occasionally on these quieter days, Allan shared with me some of the more personal details of his life, the sort of information a grandfather might tell a grandchild curious to know what life was like in 'the olden days'. With Allan no longer here to ask, these same, simple details have today taken on a slightly different significance, and grandchildren now grown-up find themselves considering questions they wish they had asked. So for them might I digress a moment?

Allan MacArthur, son of Lewis and Jenny MacArthur, was born in the Codroy Valley on May 12, 1884 in the settlement once known as MacDale. The location of his birthplace is now part of the section of Upper Ferry, and the name MacDale is forgotten by most or has never been known to any but the old people. According to Mrs. MacArthur, MacDale was so-called because the land there was taken by a closely-knit group of Scottish settlers, mostly MacArthurs and MacIsaacs, who made their homesteads there. MacDale ceased to be known by that name when the small Post Office once operated in MacArthur's home went out of use.

By today's standards, most people would consider Lewis and Jenny MacArthur's family a large one. Allan recalled that: "There was only fourteen in the family, that's all; there was ten brothers and four sisters." Life was not easy in those early days, and the parish records show numerous deaths due to diphtheria in the 1880s. Several of the MacArthurs' fourteen children died in infancy or childhood, and of those who survived four were older than Allan and four were younger. The earliest episode of his life which Allan related was that he himself almost died of diphtheria when he was only two years old. Were it not for his sister Margaret "who thought so much" of him, and who saved him from choking, he would never have lived to retell his family history and the Scottish traditions of the Valley. As it turned out, Allan outlived all of his brothers and sisters.

The children in those days knew a different kind of life from that of children today. Allan recalled when he first started school:

> I was nine years old, and I couldn't understand a word of English then, couldn't understand a word of English. I'd know "yes" and "no"—that was all.

As in the Highlands and Islands of Scotland, in those days (and even for decades later) those in authority to appoint teachers gave no consideration to the fact that most of the children to be taught were Gaelic-speakers. According to the Inspectors' Reports it was the deliberate policy of the Scottish Education Department to appoint someone from outside the area who spoke only English, someone who made no attempt to learn Gaelic, someone who expected the pupils to conform immediately to the ways of the outsider. Margaret MacArthur (Allan's daughter-in-law), a teacher from the east coast of Newfoundland, noted that appointments were made without even a mention of the fact that the children to be taught could not speak English. Children adapted easily and soon learned a new language, but this must have been the earliest death-blow to the Gaelic (and indeed to the French) language in the Codroy Valley, for there was no Trans Canada Highway in those days that could be blamed for bringing the compromise. Allan remembered the first year he went to school, around 1893:

Oh, the teachers at that time, they were from what we call Corner Brook, or Bay of Islands.[7] It was a woman teacher, the first one I went to—Mrs. MacIsaac; she was married to John MacIsaac who died. Her [maiden] name was...well, we used to call her Miss Kenny.

When asked if she had Gaelic, Allan replied, "No, no. She was Irish [Newfoundland-Irish]; she couldn't understand it." He went on to describe the early school in greater detail:

The school at that time was at Upper Ferry. The school that I went to, it was tore down years ago. I guess it was tore down around 1912 [when a new school was built in the same place]. The other one [the old school] was only small; it might have been twenty-four feet long or something like that, and perhaps twenty feet wide, no more. No, it wasn't twenty feet wide—it might have made sixteen.... It wasn't ten months of school like it is now; it was only in the wintertime and late in the fall that they'd have school. Well, you'd have to be working in the summertime, planting and weeding, and haymaking, and jigging [for codfish], and everything like that. Well, the children had to work, too. When you'd be eight or ten years of age you'd have to be out working.... Oh, I think I quit going to school when I was around fifteen, I think. I didn't go to school very much; I had to work. I was only around fifteen when I started out working.

From that time on, Allan worked at various occupations and in several different places. During the first nine or ten of these years, he worked in the area of the Valley. Much of this time was spent on his father's farm, but for part of the time he worked on the railroad.

Allan recalled the time when "around the age of twenty-four or twenty-five" he left Newfoundland and went first to Cape Breton and later to the United States:

I worked over in Cape Breton; I worked in the coal mines and I worked on construction work, among the mines in Cape Breton. Well, not all of them, only in Glace Bay.... Not out in Waterford or those places; there was no mines in my time in Waterford. They were starting the road to start a mine in Waterford—that would be in 1907, around there.

And from Cape Breton I went to Bangor [Maine] and from Bangor I went to Ellsworth, and from Ellsworth out to Bar Harbour Islands—nine miles out to sea, you know, from Ellsworth. I was working on the nursery there—a nursery of plants, you see, out in Bar Harbour Island. That was in 1908.

Oh yes, I liked it. It was really fine. Well, it was a nursery of plants, and in the fall of the year we used to dig trees...well Christmas trees, and they used to ship them to New York and Philadelphia and all those places for Christmas trees. We'd be digging them... the trees probably would be oh, around seven or eight years old, or something like that, and we had to dig them, you know, with the lifter, and we'd have burlap [hemp sacking] and put it on the ground, and then get wet moss and put it there. and then lay the tree on that and they'd gather this around and tie it with marline [twine], you see. One year we lifted fourteen hundred trees, and they were shipped out like that. Oh, it was all right... and we'd have to go out to a place called Picket Mountain—that was three miles from the nursery —with a horse and a...well, two horses and a...kind of trailer, and the woods were so far apart you could drive the horses through the woods everywhere. And the leaves used to be about, oh, about a foot thick or more, and we used to be raking up the leaves and make up the road, and then the team would take that out to the nurseries, you know, packing it away...those plants that they'd be shipping:

So, I think it was in the fall, in November... no! in December, I think it was in 1909, I left and came home and I stayed home ever since. Well, my father took sick then, and there was no...the boys were gone, so I stayed home with my father and mother. That's what happened.

On his return to the Valley, Allan took over the responsibility of his father's farm, and from then on the house he had grown up in became the home he was to live in for the rest of his life. A few months after Allan came home, his father died. According to the church records, Lewis MacArthur, age seventy, born in Cape Breton, died of cancer on April 3, 1910.

On February 12, 1913 Allan MacArthur, then twenty-eight years old, married Cecilia MacNeil, age seventeen, also of Upper Ferry. He spoke very briefly and quietly of his first marriage, which ended in the death of his young wife only seven years later. Allan and Cecilia MacArthur had four children: Lewis, James (Jim), Francis (Frank), and Loretta. Only a few months after Loretta was born in 1921, Cecilia died at the age of twenty-four, the tragic result of the absence of medical help in a time when complications in childbirth often proved fatal.

Allan's mother who of course was still at the family homestead (and remained there until her death in 1931) was a tremendous help to him in those difficult days, especially in caring for his young children. Allan was very much involved in the upbringing of his family, though from all accounts he was generally regarded as a strict father with clearly defined demands on his children. Working together as a family was, as Frank said, important to Allan:

He believed in work. He felt that people should work, and that we should be working. If there was work to be done, he believed that it should be done. Of course, there was another reason for that: I think he felt that if you worked you provided something for yourself and something for everyone.

Allan was not, however, rigid in his attitude, and was obviously closely involved with his family both in the home and outside of it:

Of course at those times the young boys, and sometimes the young girls too, though not together now, would go out down to the river here, and go for a swim. And if we were weeding, let's say myself and Jimmy and Lewis, and if there wasn't much to be done, you'd probably stay out there an hour. But even if he [father] was with us, picking up rocks, weeding, something like that, in the early afternoon, it'd be a warm day, and if we said, "Could we go for a swim?" you know there was no barrier there.... Go on for a half hour or so. Well then, we'd come back and get at the weeding or picking up rocks again. [Laughter]

The image of Allan MacArthur as the strict father disappeared when his children recalled how he used to put them to bed when they were young. Frank laughed heartily as he remembered this feature of his early childhood:

I remember...I was pretty small, I guess, then. I'd go in and my father would be teaching me my prayers at my bedside and then, when my prayers would be over [he'd say:] "Falbh ruisgte 's thig mallachd! Go naked and evil will come! Falbh ruisgte 's thig mallachd." And he'd laugh at that, you know!

At the age of thirty-nine Allan remarried. The Parish records note that he "married Mary MacDonald, age twenty-seven, of Little River [St. Andrews], on May 22, 1923." Mary then assumed the role of mother to the four children. The attitude of her stepchildren was one of love and respect. One of her stepsons, Frank, considered that he could have chosen no better himself:

We were lucky, you know, when the second time Father got married. Now lots of times, well, the stepmother she usually don't think too much of the other kids. But we were lucky that way.

Mary was as warm-hearted to her newly-acquired family as she was to her own eight children (*right*). Frank's wife added that "anyone who wouldn't get along with Mrs. MacArthur wouldn't get along with himself."

A gentle, caring woman known affectionately to all their grandchildren as 'Grandma MacArthur', Mary often appeared to be much quieter than Allan, though she had a wonderful sense of humour and a quick wit which complemented that of her husband. Characteristic of Scottish Highland women, Mary's attitude in her home clearly acknowledged her husband as head of the household and, as such, the authority on most of their traditions. After Allan's death in September 1971, however, Mary took over the role of tradition-bearer in her home, and only then did she assume the authority of passing on some of the traditions which they had shared with the other Codroy Valley Scots. She kept a diary of important events, and although this written record was a totally different approach to preserving the accuracy of information than Allan employed, she very clearly shared his love for detail and preciseness. She was an excellent correspondent and as certain details occurred to her during the years she outlived her husband, Mary would write to me, offering interesting information along with local and family news. The pattern we had established of having a ceilidh together, either at the MacArthur home or at that of family or friends, continued each long summer I spent in the Valley.

The MacArthur family in 1931: Allan is bending down in the foreground with a small child, while Mary, holding baby, is sitting on the right.

While Allan was with us there were many memorable ceilidhs that affirmed the age-old traditions which characterized Gaelic Scotland. Certainly there were changes brought about by modern transport and technology.

There were times when we shared outings by car; a delight for the driver to be asked and an obvious pleasure to the MacArthurs whose days had been those of the horse and trap. "'S dòcha gun téid sinn air chéilidh an diugh.... [Perhaps we'll go for a ceilidh today....]" was Allan's way of putting the suggestions, such as when we went to visit a friend whom he hadn't seen "since the last funeral." Sandy Francis (that is, Sandy, son of Francis—the Anglicised form of the Gaelic patronym widely used among Scots, French, Irish and English) lived in St. Andrews, and his wife had a fine reputation for barbering. If circumstances permitted perhaps we could avail of her expertise, but if not there were several other options we could take, and we'd certainly enjoy the outing to the MacIsaacs, regardless (*below*).

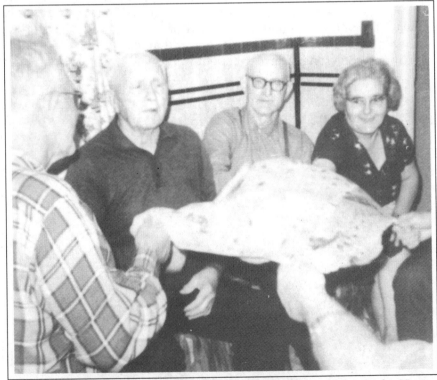

Singing a milling song at a ceilidh in Sandy Francis's house: left to right, Hector (Francis) MacIsaac; Allan MacArthur; Sandy (Francis) MacIsaac; Mrs. Kate MacIsaac (Sandy's wife), 1970.

Allan setting out to fetch home wood, 1960.

The outward trip was to be via Loch Lomond; on the dirt road where Allan had so often driven his horse and trap, along the same route he had cut and piled up many a winter's wood supply (*above*). He had watched the settlement of Loch Lomond grow from its infancy, over eight decades of land cleared gradually and brought to cultivation. He sang every verse of the song "Loch Lomond," softly punctuating it with occasional observations about points of interest, and had already suggested that "you could come home the other [coastal] road if you like, and we'll see the big land clearing that Leo has started down by the Block."

Unexpected as it was, our visit was met with the warmest of welcomes, an immediate invitation to come in, have some tea, and maybe a 'dram'. Gaelic was obviously the language of the MacIsaac home too and, just as in the Highlands of Scotland, the old folks reverted immediately to the mother-tongue, only to return politely to English upon the appearance of a non-Gaelic speaking neighbour. Before long, several neighbours had gathered to join the ceilidh, for no doubt some of them had seen their old friends, the MacArthurs, arrive. Little goes unnoticed and in any case, neighbours were glad of the opportunity to visit with the MacArthurs, who in advancing years seldom ventured far from their own garden.

Five hours later, after two haircuts, frequent pots of tea with home baking, a few drams with accompanying toasts, and conversation to catch up on several months news, Allan quietly observed that it was "after getting late, time to go home, boys." We left for home with tape recordings of numerous songs by the old folks, over twenty-five fiddle tunes, and several toasts. The music, step-dancing, conversation and laughter continued while Allan picked up an earlier thread "We'll just take a look at Leo's new land now."

This particular unplanned ceilidh could only have turned out the way it did because of the presence of approximately seven people in their seventies and eighties who were not confined to a specific work schedule or to the responsibilities of their land, responsibilities that had been taken over by younger members of their families. There was another side to the unplanned ceilidhs which I had seen many times, mostly at those in the MacArthurs' home: there was usually an impression of busyness, with the traffic back and forth from the kitchen to the livingroom or even inside and outside the house as the family attempted to get on with tasks that had been started or had to be done. Most of the time Allan sat with the visitors, having reached an age in his life when he considered himself exempt from the numerous tasks his sons were there to take over. He allowed himself the time to enjoy the company he had, as he loved to have an opportunity to participate in conversation and music which reminded him of the old days in the Valley.

Like the hard-working people in the Valley today, in his younger days his role at such a ceilidh would have been different. If someone called at a neighbour's house during the day to have a ceilidh, it would not follow that the people in the house being visited would put down their work simply to socialize. In by-gone days especially, there was far too much work for that, with butter-churning and baking to be done, carding, spinning, knitting, and weaving, along with cobbling, harness-making or any other work done by the men, to say nothing of all the outdoor work in which they all had to take a share. Those in the house would simply carry on the work; they would keep an eye on the tasks at hand and their ears to their visitor while taking it in turns to pay some additional attention to him. If the man of the house were at home, he would usually attend to the drink while the woman would offer tea and something to eat. If a ceilidh had been planned in advance, however, it was generally in the evening when the host would be prepared to spend all his time socializing with the guests. The exceptions were the occasions when the planned ceilidh was to take the form of a spinning bee or a milling [waulking]. Then all would work, guests and hosts alike.

Aside from spinning bees, most organized ceilidhs were held in the evening during the late autumn and through the winter, when the days were shorter and there was much less time to be spent doing outside work. The women, of course, did not have the same limitations of daylight hours on all their chores, as there was always work they could do, even while visitors were in the house (*below*).

As Charles W. Dunn stated in his definitive study of the Scottish Gael in Nova Scotia: "When the dusk of evening crept over the land and the tasks of the day were abandoned, the people gathered at the home of the most talented local entertainer."[8] It is not surprising then that almost all the ceilidhs I attended were in the home of Allan MacArthur which, for three generations, had been a meeting place for all who were interested in the activities of the ceilidh.

Gaelic was unquestionably the language in which Newfoundland Scots kept alive all their oral traditions, and regardless of all modern changes this fact was always evident in Allan MacArthur. Despite his strong preference for Gaelic over English, this preference did not influence Allan's attitude toward people of other language groups or cultures, for he and his family

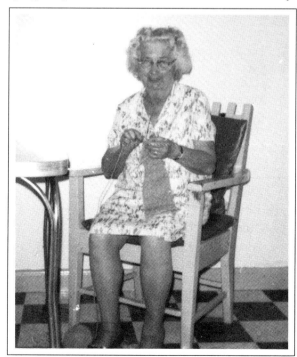

Mary MacArthur enjoying a ceilidh in her own kitchen, 1972. She is sitting in "Allan's chair."

socialized with the English, French, and Irish, along with the Scots. All were welcome in his home, for Allan MacArthur had a liking for people.

Apart from being recognized in his community for his wonderful memory, his music, and his stories, Allan MacArthur was known as well for his wit and his sense of humour. I recall one afternoon in his home when a group of young men were discussing the coming winter's wood-cutting. One of them tried to tease the old man by asking him if he would be going with them to cut wood. "No," Allan replied, "but I'll be there to measure the cords after you have it all cut." Known for his way with words, there are many other similar stories of his witty, sharp retorts. And although circumstances forced him to speak English latterly, he was quite aware of the finer shades of meaning of some words he occasionally used to catch people unawares. This was not so that he could have the satisfaction of "getting one over" on anyone, but it was rather a reflection of his continual attention to detail. For example, there was one occasion when Allan introduced a song "Oran nam Mogaisean" [The Song of the Moccasins] his brother had created many years ago, then sang the song. After he finished singing, I asked him if his brother had written many songs, to which he replied, "He never wrote a song." When I objected with "Well, he composed that one!" Allan drew my attention to my own inaccuracy in the first instance by saying, "Well, he did, he *composed* it, but he didn't *write* it, you see. He couldn't write Gaelic, you see."

Since Allan's death in 1971, individuals recall with affection the many instances when he delighted company with his vitality. People love to tell of their own special memories of him, for he was fondly regarded by the entire Valley, very much as a social being—someone with whom to spend an evening of conversation and wit, music and song; the one who would immediately come to mind when planning a party or a celebration; someone the school children could rely upon to play the bagpipes at their special events; and always the one to ask for details of the Scottish history or culture in the Codroy Valley. As far as Allan was concerned, he described himself simply and aptly: "I like company, and I like music, and I like songs and everything" (*right*).

At virtually all the evening ceilidhs, and occasionally at some daytime ones as well, the visitors would be offered a drink. If someone happened to call when there was no alcoholic beverage in the house, the host would make an apology to his visitor for being caught with nothing to offer him. He would not feel any obligation, however, since no advance notice was given. It was also customary for visitors to bring a drink to the house they visited in order that they might be able to reciprocate after they had finished the first with their host.

The first drink usually elicited a toast from one of the company, frequently one of the older men. Among the Scots, and even from French and English, the toast *slàinte mhath* (good health) was often heard. Allan MacArthur had several toasts he used as he raised his glass to all that were in the room with him. One that he frequently used was:

Scotland thy mountains
Thy valleys and fountains
The home of the poets
The birthplace of songs!

Sometimes after a few drinks he would raise his glass as if about to make a toast to his company but then would say, laughingly:

When I'm dead and in my grave
For no more whisky will I crave
But on my tomb those letters wrote:
"Many's the glass went down his throat!"

Allan, with sons Dan, George, and Martin, and daughter Margaret, 1957.

While these were toasts which he would recite for anyone who was in his company there was, however, one toast which he kept for his compatriots alone. Repeating what he had heard from the first Scottish settlers, he would raise his glass and say with feeling:

"Deoch-slàinte a' chuairtear a ghluais bho Albainn!"
[Here's a health to the traveller who left Scotland!][9]

And on one occasion when there happened to be a non-Gaelic speaker in the company he apologized, saying:

"I'm sorry that you don't understand nothing [of what I'm saying] but I'm going back to Scotland with that toast, you see, to my own people in Scotland."

Observing these social gatherings, particularly in the evening, the pattern is virtually identical to that in Scotland, where alcohol plays a significant part at the ceilidh. It is the accepted custom that most of the men and some of the women who so wish would have a 'drop' to drink or bottle of beer beside them. The ceilidh offered an opportunity for people to drink in an acceptable setting; and even those who did not drink, or drank very little, would frequently welcome the fact that certain members of the community who were known to be good musicians, singers, or dancers could more easily be persuaded to perform after they'd had 'a wee dram'.

In the Valley a ceilidh frequently was organized to celebrate a special occasion such as a birthday or a wedding anniversary, and a bottle or two of whisky or rum would be bought to help celebrate. Allan MacArthur told of one such ceilidh when a close friend of his made him a birthday gift of a wooden armchair. From that time on, Allan always sat in that chair by the kitchen table (see page 71).

While the celebration of birthdays and anniversaries among adults may seem commonplace to many, this particular consideration of family and friends infinitely surprised me since I had never heard of these annual celebrations in my own Scottish Highland Presbyterian background, which was the general pattern throughout the Highlands and Islands of Scotland. My mother, for example, did not receive a birthday card until she had left her home on the Isle of Skye, and her parents reached the age of eighty before they had a birthday remembered with a card or a gift. To ignore birthdays was the general pattern throughout the Highlands and Islands of Scotland. Allan was quick to point out that a special event like a birthday was not necessary for a ceilidh, as the simple desire to get together with family and friends was occasion enough.

A ceilidh of the kind that was planned in advance with the 'word sent around' was considered 'good' by those who attended if they spent an evening at a home where there was a moderate or even sumptuous supply of food, plenty of drink, and as many songs, stories, and lively tunes on the fiddle, guitar, mandolin, accordion, and bagpipes, with the most ostentatious show of step-dancing, that could possibly be packed into the one night. The custom of 'men in one room and women in another' observed at house parties (or 'times' as they were usually called) in certain other areas of the island is not encountered in the Codroy Valley, although the women, of course, had always spent some time in the kitchen preparing the food which was to be served.

When everyone had gathered at the house and had been served with a drink, the first half hour or so was usually spent in conversation with friends and neighbours, catching up with each other's news or telling amusing anecdotes they had heard since they last met. Before long, and usually with very little persuasion, someone would strike up a tune on one of the musical instruments. In no time at all then, the entertainment would be in 'full swing'. The bagpipes were always thought of as being a good instrument for 'getting in the mood', setting the right atmosphere, or in some instances were a good-natured method of 'shutting some people up' so they could all 'get the thing [ceilidh] off the ground' (below).

Allan and Mary MacArthur, enjoying a few tunes on the pipes, 1970.

Various instruments were thought more suitable for certain purposes. The bagpipes were regarded as the best instrument for an old-fashioned eight-hand reel and for 'set' (square) dancing. The accordion, while good for these old dances, was especially well-liked for old-fashioned waltzes. The fiddle, also suitable for any kind of dance performed in those days, however, was the favourite instrument of the step-dancers, as its volume did not overwhelm and drown out the percussion effects of feet on the wooden floors (*right*).

To any Newfoundlander familiar with the enormous wealth of traditional music with its undeniably Irish flavour, a visit to the Codroy Valley would seem like stepping into another musical world. Distinctively Scottish, with the inclusion of strathspeys (unknown elsewhere in Newfoundland) among the many reels and jigs, the choice of melody speaks volumes about the people who play so skilfully. Many of the tunes were brought over from Scotland in the mid-1800s, and along with them are Gaelic airs and waltzes picked up "across in Cape Breton" or via the Sydney radio station. Favourites include strathspeys such as "Calum Crùbach" or "Tom Dey," played in a medley with such tunes as "Muileann Dubh" or "Lord MacDonald's Reel." Waltzes such as the familiar "Cailin mo Rùinsa" are known to everyone, Gaelic speaking or not, and can be heard in medleys that include all the old Gaelic favourites, with occasional surprise inclusions of popular English songs (such as "By the Shade of the Old Apple Tree"), which just happen to fit the rhythm.

At any organized ceilidh in the Valley there was always a strictly observed code of ethics among the musicians, dancers, and singers. Just as it would be considered impolite if one person took over an entire evening's conversation, scarcely allowing anyone else to speak—not to mention boring for those who had to listen—so also would it be considered rude if a musician or singer 'hogged the whole show'. No matter how popular the music, songs, or dancing of one performer might have been, he always called a halt of his own accord, and in so doing would invite another performer to 'take his turn'. Those who were not performing were also expected to show courtesy. While the prospect of disapproval by the others was generally enough control over behaviour, on a few occasions one of the elderly men in the company gave a quite sharp reprimand to those who were rude enough to talk aloud while someone was singing a song.

Step-dancing, which people from other parts of the island often say is performed in 'different style' in the Valley to what they usually see, has always been extremely popular at a ceilidh. Since they have not seen it in Scotland, it is not unusual for Scottish visitors to the

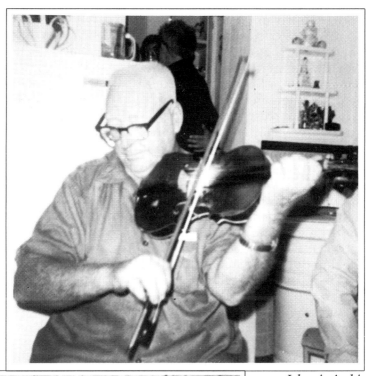

*Johnnie Archie
MacDonald
(brother of Mary
MacArthur) at a
ceilidh, 1970.*

*Frank MacArthur,
on the accordion,
with his brother
John, 1970.*

Codroy Valley or Cape Breton to assume that this step-dancing has been 'invented in North America'. This conclusion does not follow, however, as the old style of step-dancing which exists in the New World is something much older than the Highland Dancing popularized in Scotland and standardized by the Scottish Official Board of Highland Dancing and Military Regiments, who taught it during more recent years. At any rate, the testimony of the Scots in the Codroy Valley and in Cape Breton bears witness to the continuity of this old form of dancing said to have been brought over to the New World, where it survived after its disappearance from Scotland.

At any ceilidh the step-dancers would generally listen to a tune or two on the fiddle before getting out on the floor. Usually two or four people got out in the middle of the floor, and with the rest of the company sitting or standing around the edges of the room ready to watch every move, the dance would begin. Facing one another, the step-dancers would start with one of their least spectacular steps. As the music got livelier to the encouraging shouts of "Suas e! Suas a bhodaich!" the dancers would not only dance more quickly to keep up with the music, but would also progress to the most complicated steps they knew. This phrase, "Suas e! Suas a bhodaich!" still heard in the Valley even though it is now almost entirely English-speaking, is addressed to the fiddler. Used when the fiddler is being encouraged to step up the tempo of his music, the phrase translates literally as "Up with it! Up with it, old man!" Its equivalent in other areas of Newfoundland would be "Heave it outa ya, ol' man!"

While the dancers might start off doing the same step, each danced the sequence of steps of his own choice trying all the while to out-do the other dancers, not only in style and complexity but also in stamina. Throughout the dancing there would be shouts of encouragement and praise to the dancers and to the fiddler, who could always play as long as any dancer could last out on the floor. The entire show of step-dancing would come to an end after all but one dancer, usually the best one, would sit down out of fatigue, thus voluntarily eliminating themselves from the display. The dancer who was left would dance one or two solo steps and then, like the others before him, would sink into a chair laughing. Simultaneously, the fiddler would draw the last few strokes of the bow over the strings and everyone would applaud, praising the dancers with comments like, "Well, by golly, he's good," or sometimes clapping him on the back saying, "Well done, yourself."

Allan MacArthur had a life-long interest in dancing, and even into his eighties he still step-danced to the lively music at a ceilidh. His contemporaries could be heard making such remarks as, "By Gosh, he was good in his day, boy!" while Allan's own great pride was in watching his son, Frankie, dancing. Frankie, in fact, has for many years been the pride of the entire Codroy Valley when it comes to dancing. He has won the All-Newfoundland Step-Dancing Competition, has from time to time been invited to dance in Cape Breton, home of the 'real good step-dancers', and has been guest performer at Canada's foremost folk festival, the Mariposa Festival at Toronto. Those who spoke of him remarked on the fact that "he could dance with both feet," meaning that unlike most people he could use both feet with equal accuracy and agility. They drew the comparison between this rare quality in a dancer with the rarity of finding an artist who could draw equally well with either hand. Now in his late sixties, Frankie still excites all who watch, and members of these more recent audiences can be heard to make comments such as "Gosh, he's not even out of breath, and here's me in my twenties.... Nobody can beat him, boy!" There were many people in the Valley who praised Frankie MacArthur's dancing, and no doubt aware of this, his quietly modest father did not sing the praises of his own son or, in fact, even mention him when he spoke of step-dancing:

> And they knowed a lot of steps here, because we had people here that taught step-dancing, the Scots dancing. And the women, mind you, some of them was good too. There was one woman here, she was a MacDonald, she could dance sixty steps, different steps, and it was all the right dancing, you know, taught by step-dancers. Oh, I tell you, they were pretty lively. And there was good violin players here a long time ago. Well, they were teached over in Cape Breton, in Inverness, and all around those places. They knowed the tunes, a lot of them from Scotland, you see, who came out there and they followed the tunes from Scotland right down.

Instrumental music was not, however, the only accompaniment for dancing. As Allan MacArthur said, "Some of the step-dancing tunes they used to be in Gaelic." Just as in the Highlands and Islands of Scotland, these tunes in Gaelic, *puirt-a-beul* or 'mouth-music' as they were generally called, were very popular in the Valley and were referred to as *puirt luath* by the Gaelic speakers. Since this type of singing required exceptional breath control in order to sing long enough for a step-dancer, there were never more than a few people in the Valley at the one time who had mastered this art. Consequently, during the joint performance of mouth-music and step-dancing, the audience at the ceilidh were doubly excited, watching the feet of the dancer and listening to the accuracy of the singer who, if he took a breath in the wrong place or for a split second too long, might lose the beat and spoil the entire effect. In Allan's own repertoire were well-known Gaelic favourites such as a variant of "Mrs. MacLeod of Raasay" sung as "Bodachan a Mhirean."

Mouth music had another function, however, and that was to teach a piper or violin player a new tune. Most of the musicians, including Allan MacArthur, could not read music. If they wanted to learn a new tune they memorized and played by ear. A musician could assimilate some tunes into his repertoire simply because he heard them repeatedly, but there were many instances when a conscious effort was made to learn a new tune. And where better to do so than at a ceilidh! There Allan, like virtually every piper in Scotland, had sat down and learned tunes from the singing of a fellow musician:

> A lot of them tunes that they played, the old people, a lot of them here, those that used to play music anyhow, they used to know them in Gaelic, you see. They would sing it and then play it for step-dancing:
>
> When you know the words and the air of that, that's just as good as the notes, pretty near. I couldn't play by note but by ear, you see. But for fast tunes, and the old tunes, and when you know the Gaelic words of it, well you had the run of it if you were to keep time for the step-dance.

Allan providing the music for a wedding, c.1958.

Allan was also familiar with the pipers' special syllable language for transmitting a new tune, namely *canntaireachd* which he demonstrated when the occasion demanded it. He knew the great importance of having a tune first of all firmly in the mind before transferring it to the chanter or the pipes (see example of this syllabic notation on page 142).

Entertainment at the ceilidh was not all loud and lively with music and dancing. There was also a place for serious songs, and indeed they were often a welcome change of pace. It was usually at a ceilidh that the songs which were not work songs could be heard, such as the old narrative and heroic songs from Allan MacArthur's mother's repertoire: "She had a lot of songs with no chorus in them, like war songs—as well as the milling songs, that is."

Apart from the old songs which told stories, no ceilidh was complete without several good stories. In fact, there were many ceilidhs at which the emphasis was almost solely upon storytelling. There were also a few people who, if they were present, would always be called upon to perform at least one of the recitations from their repertoire. The people in the early days especially had a great love of hearing and telling stories—of the land they left behind them, of their pioneer days in the land they came to settle, of adventures on the high seas or in the lumber woods, and, of course, the many aspects of the supernatural which were always of interest to the Scottish Highlanders the world over.

Although the original ceilidh as Allan and his contemporaries knew it is now a thing of the past, the concept of the ceilidh is still with the Codroy Valley people. An impromptu visit is still welcomed warmly, with spontaneous comments such as that of Frank's wife, Margaret: "Put the darned old television off. We'll have a cup of tea now." At a gathering of family and friends in the Valley today, people still love to talk about how their forebears settled the land, how they healed the sick, or buried the dead. The 'real old stories', which will be dealt with in a later chapter, have now disappeared, although there is still a lively interest in retaining the pattern of conversational topics which was adopted about thirty years ago, after the generation of the first settlers had passed on. Today's ceilidhs include anecdotes of weddings and wakes; stories about the witty, wise, eccentric, and simple folk; recollections of fun-making and prank-playing; memories of the old-time milling frolics in the days when they made everything they wore; and of the days when the 'real old ceilidhs' were much more a part of their way of life. And seldom is there a ceilidh at which the name of Allan MacArthur is not included among the reminiscences and traditions of the Codroy Valley.

CHAPTER 4

Come Over by the Stove

> The wild game was plenty all round...and salmon and trout and eels and rabbits. You'd never starve.
> *Allan MacArthur, 1970*

The domestic life of the Scottish settlers in the Codroy Valley was, for the most part, a carry-over of the way of life in the Scottish Highlands of the mid-1800s. The Scottish Highlander was accustomed to the traditional stone-built croft houses, where even in the second half of this century one can find inhabited thatched houses such as those left behind by the emigrants (*right*). There were, of course, inevitable changes made to suit the conditions of the new land, such as the timber-built houses which provide sharp contrast to the old. One is immediately confronted by a general misconception that the Gaelic language and culture dwells only within the ancestral stone walls. Not so—it thrives and flourishes in borrowed fashions of wood.

The house in which Allan MacArthur spent much of his life was one of the many built at the turn of the century by carpenters from Cape Breton (*see page 25, top*). It was a two-storey house with a large kitchen and a sitting room, or 'the room' as it was called, taking up the ground floor, and stairs leading from the small hallway opposite the front door to the four upstairs bedrooms with their low walls, sloping ceilings, and dormer-type windows. The outside of the house had elaborately carved door and window mouldings, perhaps a mark of the days when tradesmen took time and care to finish their work in the neatest way they could. The chimney, set against the back

(Above): Croft houses and out buildings in Moidart, Scotland, 1959. This area is within the district from whence the MacIsaacs emigrated in the mid-1800s. (Below): Moidart, Scotland. Well over a century after many inhabitants of this area had emigrated to North America, these thatched cottages were still inhabited and the crofts still operated (School of Scottish Studies, 1959).

of the house between the kitchen and 'the room', was built by Allan MacArthur's grandfather who, when he emigrated, was a stonemason to trade, and according to his grandson, "could build any kind of a chimney."

'The room' was the name always given to the best, and seldom-used, room in the house—a sitting room where the family kept all their finest dishes, ornaments, framed pictures of their forebears, and their most elaborate holy pictures, crucifixes, and usually a very ornate Sacred Heart. (In Scotland, where it serves exactly the same purpose as in the Valley, people also refer to the best sitting room as 'the room'.) It was the special place kept for visitors, for special occasions such as weddings, or where the family would gather for their own special celebrations, or at Christmas-time. It was also the place where the dead were laid out during a wake.

This style of house which was popular at that time can still be seen in the Codroy Valley, although it is not as much in evidence there today as it is in Cape Breton. While basically still this same structure, the MacArthurs' home has been altered to a central chimney home by the addition of a very large kitchen at the back of the house and upstairs, above this, two bedrooms with a small 'box room' between. At the same time as these rooms were added, the roof was removed and the upstairs walls raised to eliminate the original dormer windows. Then with the walls of the new extension and those of the original part now all the same height, the house was roofed (*see page 25, bottom*). With seven rooms upstairs, one was turned into a bathroom. Mrs. MacArthur made two entries in her notebook of events which related to their newly-renovated house: "Started building the new kitchen June 21 1948"; and "Had dinner in it July 1st." This newer style of house, so popular in the 1940s, remained the prevalent type of two-storey house until the early 1970s.

The running of the household was solely the work of the woman of the house, although decisions to make major food and clothing purchases for the family usually required her husband's approval. A family would deal at one of the Valley's general stores, such as A.D. MacIsaac's at Upper Ferry or his brother's, Duncan MacIsaac's, at Little River (later St. Andrew's).

In the late autumn of each year the winter supplies were bought from the store, and these had to last at least until May, when spring came. Although the store remained open all winter, there were several reasons for 'buying in for the winter'. First of all, the autumn brought extra earning potential to the people of the Valley with the harvesting of blueberries, partridgeberries, marshberries and bakeapples, which could be sold to the merchant or, more likely, used for credit on purchases made. For this same purpose, the merchant also accepted vegetable crops, and Mrs. MacArthur mentioned that many families, including her own, exchanged butter and eggs along with knitted mitts and socks.

These commodities, like the berries, were shipped to markets outside the area or occasionally resold locally. Secondly, buying in supplies before the onset of winter also eliminated the possibility of a family being left without food during particularly stormy weather such as Allan MacArthur described, when even a horse could not get through the road for the deep drifts of snow. In weather conditions like that, if someone in the area needed a priest or a doctor, a group of men would clear the road in order to let a horse and sleigh get through.

Mrs. MacArthur recalled a typical list of provisions she would buy to feed her family for the winter: a fifty-pound sack of beans; a box of raisins and a box of prunes, with about ten pounds of fruit in each; a five-gallon keg of molasses; a one-hundred-pound sack of coarse Scotch oatmeal; a one-hundred-pound sack of table corn meal; seven or eight one-hundred-pound bags of flour; a one-hundred-pound bag of sugar; a one-hundred-pound sack of onions; five or more ten-pound chests of tea; a two-hundred-pound barrel each of salt turbot, salt cod, and salt herring; and a two-hundred-pound barrel of salt beef. The flour was sold in strong cotton bags, and the sugar came in a thin cotton bag packed inside a strong paper bag. Mrs. MacArthur added that she didn't like to buy very much tea from the local store because she "didn't like the tea they used to have; it was cheap tea they had, and it smelled like hay boiling on the stove." Instead, she would wait for an opportunity to buy some from Channel (Port aux Basques).

Since most families required such large quantities of provisions from the store it was not surprising that many found it difficult to pay, and as a result found themselves bound to the general merchant by an almost perpetual debt. Mrs. MacArthur described the system of credit:

> The shopkeeper used to mark it down, so you wouldn't have to pay all at once. They'd keep it in the books, and whenever you'd have so much [money or exchangeable goods] you'd always have to give it to them, and you'd never have any [cash] to spare.

In spite of this system, the people in the Codroy Valley still considered themselves a lot more fortunate than most Newfoundlanders, for they were better able to use their land to produce crops, livestock, and dairy products than the people living in other parts of the island. This was especially noticeable during the Depression years of the 1930s. Mrs. MacArthur added:

> We used to have our own meats salted [in brine] as there was no way of keeping it fresh then. We used to kill a pig that would weigh over 260 pounds and salt it, and also a couple of sheep, and salt that.

When slaughtering animals, certain traditions were always followed and are still kept by most people to this day. A pig was always slaughtered two or three days after the new moon "because the pork will taste better and the meat won't shrink when you cook it." This custom, which was also prevalent throughout Scotland, was affirmed by one of the MacArthurs who had just killed a pig prior to my visiting them. His wife was frying some of this pork and showed me that it did not shrink; however, she pointed out that they had once killed the pig at the wrong time and it "just went away to nothing in the pan." The Scottish people in the Valley never saved the pig's blood when slaughtering, but the French people did and used it for making blood puddings. When asked why the Scottish did not save it, Mrs. MacArthur said she did not know; however, a woman of French ancestry made the comment that the Scots would not save it because they said the Devil went through it. The French also ate the pork liver while the Scots discarded it. They seemed to give no reason for this, except that this is what the old people always did. For this same reason they continued to eat the liver of lamb and beef and some of the game animals, discard kidneys of all animals, discard pig's head while they cooked sheep's and cow's head, and yet used the hearts of all these animals.

Although they made all their own butter in the summer, they could not do so in the winter when the cows went dry. Mrs. MacArthur commented that there was no such thing as margarine in those days, "only the good butter," and in order to keep the family supplied they had to salt a tub or two, each containing about twenty-five or thirty pounds of butter. "When that was gone, there would be no more butter until the cows would freshen in the spring."

Eggs were also very scarce in winter, for the colder the weather became the fewer eggs the hens would lay. In the late autumn Mrs. MacArthur would "put away eggs in a cool place for the Christmas baking," and by the time the New Year had been celebrated, they would be almost without eggs until Easter. "When the hens would stop laying, we had no more eggs till they would start in the spring. We would be saving up for Easter Sunday. That was the big day, see how many eggs you would eat. John and George used to eat nine or ten each!" No doubt this custom (like many others) is a direct carry-over from the Highlands of Scotland where many families have enjoyed this self-same Easter treat year after year.

Needless to say, with all these basic supplies purchased for the winter, the woman of the house was kept busy preparing virtually everything the family ate. To the modern housewife, seven or eight barrels of flour must seem an enormous amount, but it was quickly used up in the baking of bread and bannocks, *bonnach* or buttermilk cakes as they were sometimes called. Yeast was not among the items bought in the very early days, for there was none available in the Valley. Instead, people used hops to leaven their bread. Allan MacArthur described to me those days:

> Well, we used to use hops, you know, first, when the yeast wasn't plenty round here.... We used to grow hops, and then in the fall of the year we'd pick the leaves off them and pack them up, you know, for the winter. Oh yes, we used to grow hops. Well, we could buy them in pound packages, you know. And that's what they used to make the bread of before there was yeast cake.

Though many years had passed since she used hops as a leavening agent, Mrs. MacArthur recalled how it was done:

> We'd boil the hops and strain it, then boil it with a cup of molasses or sugar. Add some cooked mashed potatoes and salt. Boil it on the stove again, then thicken with flour.

From his own experience as cook in the early sporting camps (see page 89), Allan added:

> They'd probably fill a gallon jar with that, and when they'd be going to mix bread, they'd probably take a cup and a half of that and put it in. Now, that was as good as yeast.

Mrs. MacArthur gently added: "No, it wasn't as good, but it had to do."

On this same subject of bread making, Mrs. MacArthur stated she used to make bread at least twice a week when all the family were still at home. She would mix the bread at night, then cover it with a cloth and put coats and sweaters on top of it to keep it warm. She would leave it like that overnight, and by morning it would be "up right high," ready to be put into six or eight loaf pans and baked in the oven.

The MacArthurs also described how some people kept aside a small bun of dough from one baking day to use to leaven the bread on the next baking day. This they called 'sour dough'.

The Scottish women also made *bonnachs*, or 'bannocks' as they were sometimes called in English. Leavened with baking soda, or a mixture of baking soda and baking powder rather than yeast, these were usually made in large, segmented 'rounds' of about ten inches across and an inch or more thick. More recently, most people have made them in small individual portions cut out with a cup or glass from the flattened dough. In North America the *bonnach* is like a baking powder bun or buttermilk cake and is often called 'baking powder biscuit' by today's housewife; in Scotland it is the well-known oven scone. Mrs. MacArthur didn't use a written recipe —she simply mixed together a four-cup sieve of flour, one teaspoon of baking soda, a quarter pound of shortening, and some salt, along with just enough sour milk to make the dough. If sweet (fresh) milk was used, she would add two teaspoons of baking powder to the other ingredients. This would make one large *bonnach*, enough for one meal. She also saw her mother-in-law baking them on the top of the stove on an iron griddle (more usually called 'girdle'). The method is also common in Scotland, though the women of the Valley did not use the Scottish name, 'griddle scones', for this particular variation.

To me—a Scot living in Newfoundland—the food in the Codroy Valley showed a distinct Newfoundland influence with a considerable degree of uniformity of cooking habits among the Scots, French, Irish, and English alike. Favourite Newfoundland cooking practices—such as frying or roasting with salt fat-back pork added for flavour; boiling vegetables with salt-pickled or corned beef; and the popular salt 'spare ribs' boiled with vegetables, frequently turnip greens—are part of the day-to-day menus. Since I had come across none of these cooking methods in Scotland, I concluded that this was one area in which the Scots at least had adapted their traditional ways to fit the availability of certain commodities of the New World. There was one interesting exception pointed out to me by a Newfoundlander, Sidney Shears of Jeffreys, who worked in a brush-cutting camp at Morris's Brook where Allan MacArthur was the cook in the early 1950s. He noted that the Scots tended to boil their cabbage for a much shorter time than the average Newfoundlander would. Mr. Shears, who described Allan MacArthur as a "fine gentleman," said that he was "the first person ever I saw cook cabbage for only ten or fifteen minutes—and was it ever delicious! We were always used to having it completely cooked for an hour at home."

Although sheep were plentiful in the Codroy Valley, there was no sign or mention of dry-salted mutton, the primary meat dish in the Scottish Highlands and Islands even when I was growing up in the 1950s and early 1960s. When I asked Allan MacArthur about this, he was most interested in knowing how mutton was salted in

At a sporting camp: Allan MacArthur (cook) and Jack White admire the day's prize catch, 1934.

Scotland, as he had never heard of the practice of placing alternate layers of coarse salt and dry mutton in a barrel to preserve it. He did, however, point out that there was no need for such a commodity in the Codroy Valley, for if they butchered a sheep in the winter it could be kept frozen simply by storing it in an out-building during the very cold weather. In fact, he said, there was absolutely no reason other than personal preference for them to eat as much salted foods as they did, so plentiful was the wild game and fish available to them. He emphasized the fact that no one need ever go hungry in the Codroy Valley in those days, for there were plenty of hares, rabbits, caribou, and wild birds for the taking, and one needed only to go down to the river to catch salmon, trout, or eels. Besides that, most families killed their own sheep, cattle and pigs. When they did salt or pickle an animal, they did so in a briny solution, often the pickle left over from a barrel of salt meat that had been already used up.

Dairy produce was in plentiful supply all of the year except when the cows went dry during part of the winter. Milking the cows was women's work, just as it used to be in Scotland. Allan MacArthur often described his mother going to milk the cows; and judging from the number of times he repeated the description, I would assume that her approach to work was one aspect of Jenny MacArthur's character which left a deep impression upon her son:

> She never milked a cow without singing a song, and the cow would know her, and she had to be very careful when she'd go in the cow-yard because the cows knowed her so well. And she'd be singing a song for every cow she'd milk. And the cows would come to the gate, you see, and the best ones would [be milked first]. The rest would have [to wait]...my mother had to milk that one first, you see.

After the cows were milked, the warm milk was poured from the large milking pails through a sieve covered with muslin and into big bowls. There it was left to cool, the milk settling to the bottom while the cream rose to the surface. If the cream was required for butter-making it would be skimmed off the top with a saucer or a large spoon and stored in a crock until butter-making time.

Butter was usually made in an earthenware crock which, depending on the size of the family and the frequency of churning, would be between ten and twenty-four inches high. Its capacity varied from one to five gallons and its shape was either straight-sided with bevelled edge, or like a barrel. A churn was called *muidhe* by the Codroy Valley Scots. It had a wooden lid, usually home-made, and there was always a hole about an inch in diameter in the centre of the lid. The actual churning was done with a 'dasher', either a flat piece of wood or a cross-shape of wood attached at right angles to a long cylindrical wooden shaft of eighteen to thirty-six inches long and a diameter slightly less than that of the hole in the lid. If the cream stored in the crock had become so thick as to be almost solid, the woman making butter would add water to it before she churned. She would then put the long shaft down in the thick cream and place the lid on so that the shaft came up through the hole and fitted neatly into the top of the crock. Next she would work the shaft up and down rhythmically until finally it thickened and butter was made. Mrs. MacArthur usually made butter once a week in her large churn, using three or four gallons of cream, which yielded up to ten pounds of butter.

A woman would often sing songs of a suitable rhythm while churning, and this was certainly the case with the MacArthur family. Frequently the children, or whoever happened to be in the house, would take over the churning to give the housewife a rest, or to allow her to get on with some other household task requiring her attention. When the butter was ready, she would return to the churn to complete the task. She would remove the lid and the wooden shaft, scraping off any butter that had stuck to them. She then drew her hand all around the sides of the churn and through the buttermilk to gather all the butter into a large mass before removing it from the crock. The new butter then had to be washed thoroughly in cold water, squeezing it at the same time to remove all traces of buttermilk. This had to be done to keep the butter fresh, for any buttermilk left in new butter would quickly taint it. Often a little salt was then added to the butter, the amount depending on individual taste and on the length of time they hoped to keep it fresh. Finally, the butter was shaped into blocks with wooden butter-pats and stored until needed.

When butter was plentiful in midsummer, many people would sell it to tourists visiting the area. Frank remembered when as children they were expected to take part in the work involved and to comply with the high standards specified by his father, for, as far as Allan MacArthur was concerned, "if a job is worth doing, it is

George MacArthur demonstrating the use of the butter churn to the author, 1971. Above, wooden dasher for the butter churn.

worth doing well," and that principle was applied to any aspect of work:

> Making butter and selling butter was one of the sources of income. And we had a brook above the road where we got water, and below the road there was a spring. Now there was only two places where you got water. But the water in the spring below the road was much clearer and cleaner. And they were selling butter to a man in Deer Lake by the name of A.W. Morley. And when they'd be going to wash the butter, someone would have to go to the spring below the road and get the bucket and get this nice clean, clear water from out the spring; which was colder, clearer and cleaner to wash the butter to get it ready for selling. Now this is one instance, the way he [Father] wanted things done, well, you had to open one gate and cross the road, and open another gate and go to the spring and get the water and come back and open the gate...! But that was the way he wanted that water to clean the butter.

Today there are still many tourists who call in the Valley for butter, but there are only two or three women left who make it and they cannot hope to fulfil the demand that still exists. Most people who sell butter press it into pound moulds, though some of the older people did use fancy butter pats and moulds that came from Scotland.

Prior to the coming of electricity in 1962 there was, of course, no refrigeration during the summer. Since this was also the time the milk yield was highest, large quantities of milk went sour before it could be used. Fortunately, there was no loss as they used to make the sour milk into *gruth*, which is generally known as 'cottage cheese'. About two gallons of sour milk—or sometimes one gallon of separated skimmed milk with two or three cupfuls of buttermilk added and left for two or three days to become thick and sour—were put into a large pot and placed on the top of the stove, but not over direct heat, and left for several hours until it had separated out into curds and whey. The correct amount of warmth for this process was very important, for it had to be kept well below boiling point; and if the stove had to be heated up in the meantime to cook a meal, the pot of sour milk would be removed altogether and set down beside the stove with just enough heat to keep it warm. The pot full of curds and whey was then strained through a muslin cloth; the greenish liquid, the whey, was given to the pig or poured away, while the white solid, the curds, was squeezed in the muslin cloth. Salt was then added for flavour to complete the making of *gruth*, and as a special delicacy it was sometimes mixed with thick cream.

The *gruth* (or *gruth* and cream) was spread on freshly baked *bonnach* or *aran coirce*. The latter, often called 'oat-cake', is made by rolling out a mixture of coarse oatmeal, salt, baking soda (bicarbonate of soda), butter, and hot water, which is then baked on an iron griddle and toasted in front of the fire until brittle and browned. As far as I know, no one in the Valley today makes oat-cakes in the traditional manner, for when I brought some to Allan MacArthur on one occasion he said that he hadn't seen them since his mother made them more than forty years previously. Mrs. MacArthur said she had never eaten them. Perhaps the introduction of more refined foods, such as the pre-packaged rolled oats which replaced the sacks of oatmeal, has contributed to the change in eating habits. Only recently I heard the MacArthurs' son-in-law ask why he had not seen or tasted *gruth* for many years, and the reply given by Mrs. MacArthur was that people didn't bother to milk as many cows any more, and the milk from the ones that are milked is now kept refrigerated, leaving no great quantities of sour milk which is needed to make the *gruth*.

All the vegetables required for the Valley were grown by the farmers in the area. Aside from the extensive fields of fodder crops, settlers set aside land for the cultivation of vegetables and sometimes fruit. Allan MacArthur said that his family always planted their carrots and other vegetables in the 'black earth' as it produced the finest crops. The 'black earth' was the very dark, almost black, alluvial deposits found within two or three hundred yards of the Great Codroy River (*see page 44*). I have watched crops planted there for five consecutive years and have seen evidence of the wisdom of choosing this particular soil; every year they picked from it an abundance of carrots, beets (beetroot), cabbage, lettuce, cucumber, and sometimes spinach, marrows, and other vegetables. From these, the root crops and cabbage were, and often still are, stored in the cool cellar beneath the house to last till the following year's crops were ready. Since they are basic to most meals, however, potatoes and turnips are grown in such great quantities that they require individual fields solely for their cultivation. They, too, are stored in the cellar for winter.

Before the turnips developed bulbous roots the plants were thinned out and the greens eaten as an early vegetable. Within a short period of time the turnip fields yielded far more greens than could be eaten by one family; consequently, it was not uncommon for people who had no turnip crop to be invited to help themselves to the greens. This also helped the farmer, for the person picking the turnip greens for his own use also thinned out a portion of the farmer's turnip field. Today some of the local farmers sell turnip greens through the local grocery stores or by means of roadside signs, but many families keep aside enough greens to preserve in bottles for the winter when fresh vegetables are not available.

The practice of preserving foods for the winter has been common to almost all Codroy Valley kitchens for many years, regardless of ethnic background. This food preserving, or bottling, as it was usually called, began each year in the early summer with the turnip greens. Later, when the bakeapples ripened they were gathered and bottled; and from this early summer beginning, the woman of the house could expect to find herself bottling various products until the onset of winter. When observing the busy housewives coping with their preparations for the winter, it struck me as a remarkable feat of nature that the kitchen was not glutted with produce all requiring attention at the same time; rather, when the bakeapple crop had all been bottled, the wild strawberries were ripe enough to be picked and preserved. When this task was completed, flocks of children, and some adults besides, used almost every available kitchen receptacle to gather wild raspberries, a harvest which took longer corresponding to the greater quantities of this particular berry. And so it continued until autumn when the wild gooseberries, black currants, choke cherries, blueberries, plums, partridgeberries, and finally the marshberries (cranberries) had all been preserved. I collected no traditional jam or fruit preserving recipes from the Valley, as Mrs. MacArthur said that almost all the jam was made according to the pamphlets given out by the Jubilee Guild, who used to hold meetings in the Valley about the mid-1940s. Most likely the popular Jubilee Guild recipes replaced many traditional ones.

There were, however, several traditional recipes for bottling various products which have been passed down from mother to daughter over the years. When all the jam was put away, there were numerous vegetable crops which had to be preserved. Several families 'put-up' their small carrots in bottles, but the MacArthurs stored them with the larger carrots under a fine layer of sand in their cellar. Most of the cabbage was also stored there, stalk upwards, but a certain amount usually was pickled and bottled as "Cabbage Chow." Mrs. MacArthur dictated for me how to make a few bottles of cabbage chow using a recipe she had invented:

> Shred a large head of cabbage. Put it in a bowl and add a quarter of a cup of salt. Cut up six or seven onions and put them in the bowl also. Sprinkle with another quarter of a cup of salt and mix it all up together. Cover the bowl and leave it overnight. In the morning, pour off all the brine that will have collected and rinse the shredded vegetables in cold water to get most of the

salt off it. Put it in a pot with eight or nine cored, unpeeled apples —sliced up. Add a quart of vinegar and a quart of water and boil until it is cooked—about half an hour. Get about half a cup of flour and about a teaspoon of turmeric and a teaspoon of dry mustard, and a shake of salt, and a teaspoon of celery salt, and mix all together with water—just as you do when making gravy. Add this to the hot mixture on the stove and stir. Boil it for a little while until it thickens, and watch it in case it burns. Pour the chow into hot bottles and put the covers on tightly and store. You don't need to seal the jars, as they will keep just like that.

Most families with vegetable gardens also picked beets but, depending on the family, the recipes varied. Just as the bottling of garden produce was coming to an end, the housewife was usually faced with the task of bottling moose meat. The moose and caribou hunting seasons generally began in the early autumn, and before the days of refrigeration the only way to keep the meat was to bottle it. While most of the families in the Valley today are able to deep-freeze meats, Mrs. MacArthur recalled the days when everyone bottled moose, caribou, rabbits, chicken, ducks, or whatever wild meat they had and needed to preserve. She said that there was one standard method used for all meats, and dictated her own recipe:

Cut up the meat in small pieces and put it into sterile bottles. Add one teaspoon of salt and fill with water to cover the meat. Seal the jar as tight as you can, then put the bottles into a large pot, with cardboard between the bottles. Cover the bottles with cold water one inch above the tops, and boil them for two and a half to three hours. Take the bottles out and don't turn the sealer ring when it is hot, or you will break the seal, but when it is completely cooled, you can take the ring off the jar and use it again, for by then it will be sealed. Put the jars away in storage.

Despite the universality of the deep-freeze, bottled meat is still popular among the old and middle-aged people. They also enjoy 'head cheese', made from the head of either a sheep or a cow which they have slaughtered. Mrs. MacArthur described how she made head cheese:

Cut the meat off the cow's (sheep's) jaws and put this in a big pot with the tongue. Boil until the meat is tender and leave in the pot overnight. In the morning, skim off all the fat and save the liquid. Put the meat into the meat grinder and also six or seven onions. Add half a teaspoon of cloves and some pepper, and return it to the pot of liquid and boil it all together for an hour. Scald the bottles (or if they're new you have to boil them), and put one teaspoon of salt in a pint bottle or two teaspoons in a quart. Put the meat mixture in the bottles and stir to mix up the salt. Put the lids on as tight as possible and put cardboard between the bottles. [If the glass touches, the bottles will break.] Cover with cold water until it is one inch above the top of the bottles. Boil this for one and a half hours. Take the bottles out and don't turn the sealer ring or it will break the seal. You do the same thing as with bottled moose. Put away in storage.

With so many foods preserved in bottles, by the end of the autumn the storage shelves, usually in the basement or in the cold cellar beneath the house, were stocked full, ready for the long winter. During my many visits to the Valley, I saw evidence time and time again of Allan MacArthur's statement that people need never be short of food, for numerous bottles of moose, poultry, head cheese, vegetables, pickles and fruit preserves were opened for me by welcoming families who insisted that I stay to eat with them. I also received gifts of these bottles from neighbours, and often from Mrs. MacArthur who would joke that certain bottles, especially wild strawberries and bakeapples, should not be opened until December 25, for they were considered special.

Today's visitor to the Valley who stays even a few days will quickly notice an enthusiasm for homemade beverages, particularly among the men. With most of the emphasis in the Valley today upon homemade beer, there is a vast difference to the early days that the old people knew. In those days the beverages made included teas and a kind of coffee. Although they could purchase boxes of tea, as already mentioned, Allan MacArthur said that they used to make their own herbal teas at one time:

> Well, we used to grow mint, you see; and tea was scarce here then, and there was no coffee at all with the old people. Well they used to get this mint and steep it in boiling water, like you would... anything. And you'd drink that instead of tea; put milk in it, and drink it like tea. Oh, it was good. Well, if I had time I think I could get you a little bit of the wild mint yet, it's down in that place yet. It's a weed, it growed about that high [approximately one foot].

The method of infusing dill tea was similar, and Allan added that this drink was used medicinally for the treatment of pneumonia and pleurisy.

While there was no coffee to be bought in the Valley in those days, families were not without their own variety of it. According to Allan MacArthur, this recipe for coffee which was made during his youth came from "the people that came from Scotland":[1]

> Well, the loaf bread especially, that's what we used, and when it would be a couple of days old (well, fresh bread would

be no good), but when it would be getting a little stale, probably two or three days, you'd cut it about a half-inch thick, and then you'd have a good fire on, and you'd roast it, you know. It would be no good on top of the stove, you see, you wouldn't roast it. And you'd put it on the kilders [hot embers] till it would catch afire, you see, and on both sides. And when it would be black, about half-ways through, an eighth of an inch on both sides, then while it was on fire, you see, you'd have a dish of hot water, and you'd just take that out and you'd dump it in the water, when the bread was all afire. And that would give you coffee.

Non-alcoholic beverages were not, however, the only kind made in the Valley in the early days, for alcohol has always played a part in the social life of the people (*below*). Methods of procuring liquor differed in the old days, as Allan MacArthur explained during his discussion on the topic:

I can remember around seventy years ago, well they used to make beer, you know.... There was no yeast cake then at that time. They used to brew it but it wasn't very strong.... There was

Sandy Cormier pours a little refreshment for the piper, Allan MacArthur, at a summer picnic, while Freddie White (far left) and Leo Cormier look on (1950s).

no malt, just molasses; well, they used to put hops into it, you know, to work. Oh, I remember well when there was no malt to be got around here.

Well, we didn't make much beer here before 1918, the First World War, then when they came home from it and they had German receipts, you see, and other kinds of receipts for making beer, they started from that.

Allan's son, John, recalled that it was in the 1940s when store-bought malt appeared; home-brewed beer then became popular in the Valley. Allan saw no need to elaborate on any recipe— the instructions are clearly enough printed on the tins of malt. Occasionally, however, some modifications were made, such as adding extra sugar so that the yeast would 'work off' faster than stated on the recipe, or adding a large can of apple juice to improve the taste and disguise the smell of yeast.

The practice of modern home-brewing, however, seems insignificant compared to the earlier days of smuggling from the French island of St. Pierre, off the south coast of Newfoundland, or to the old times when it was customary to produce 'a little bit of moonshine'. Those days are now regarded as long past, and if the occasional sip of 'shine appears, "Gosh, it must have come across from Cape Breton!"

It was not simply the implications of the 'illicit still' that put people off the idea of distilling their own alcohol. In 1971, when Allan MacArthur reflected that he "didn't make any moonshine since thirty years," he gave his own sound reasons for stopping:

> Oh well, we were getting the rum from St. Pierre; it wasn't worth while, and it was much better, you know, because this alcohol, it was no good for a person—too strong, too much alcohol.

He made a passing reference to the paraphernalia with the little copper pipe that had not been seen on his stove for many a long year; the clear drops of liquid that slowly emerged so strong they could sustain a flame on a spoon; the sugar burned to sticky caramel in order to colour the desired product, and with that little glimpse, Allan closed the subject, leaving little doubt that while he once had the expertise, passing it on was not a priority.

Of greater historical interest to Allan were the days of the rum-running, well within his own memory:

> People used to go down to St. Pierre and smuggle rum, smuggle whisky, smuggle brandy, smuggle Troix-Six [possibly Triple-Sec?] and every kind of stuff like that. And it was cheap 'cos they used to get it from France, you see, beer and wine and

whisky, and every kind of stuff like that. Well, it was a lot cheaper than what the beer is today, a lot cheaper.

Although never in St. Pierre himself, Allan could tell about the days when it was common for people from the Valley to go to St. Pierre in schooners:

> A fifty-ton schooner, a hundred-ton schooner, from that down to a twenty-four ton schooner, they used to go down there. They'd go down to Fortune Bay, you know, selling potatoes, and St. Pierre is right in the mouth of Fortune Bay.
>
> You would get a bottle of gin for twenty-five cents and that would be stronger than the eight dollar rum you get today [1971]. Well, you'd get that for about a dollar-fifty a gallon, or something like that.

He recalled the most popular drinks of those days:

> Oh, they used to drink a lot of whisky, and gin and brandy, and a lot of rum too. Maybe not so much of rum as they used to drink. They used to drink a lot of gin that used to come from France, and the brandy too.

With the advent of the Newfoundland Board of Liquor Control, however, smuggling soon became a thing of the past:

> And then they got started from St. John's, you know, selling rum. They were getting it in, the government took a hold of it, and then they had to turn against St. Pierre, you see. They had to put force [police patrol boats] on for to be chasing those that used to go from all around the Island—go to St. Pierre for this rum, and the rum that the government was getting wasn't getting the sale, you see. And it cost them millions of dollars to do that.

In 1966 the paving of the Trans Canada Highway brought easy access to the Bond Store [Board of Liquor Control] in Port aux Basques, a mere twenty-five minute drive away. Now, in the 1980s, that department has opened a branch in the Codroy Valley, under the current name of the Newfoundland Liquor Commission, making it all the easier to obtain the once elusive beverages.

Nevertheless, several families still continue to brew beer, and many also make wine, just as the old folk did in years gone by when nature offered them an ample supply of basic ingredients. Their winemaking was usually done around September when the blueberries were plentiful, or when their own garden of blackcurrants produced a good crop of fruit. Allan recalled briefly how they used to make it:

We used to make blueberry wine. We put a gallon or two of them in a dish and put water and molasses on that. We put yeast in it for to 'work'—well, we used to use hops first, when the yeast wasn't plenty around here—and leave it to brew up, then you had blueberry wine. It would be kind of thick but not very thick, but a little thicker than water.

In recent years, the 'dish' in which the wine was made has been a large earthenware urn, holding about five gallons, once the family butter churn (*see page 91*). When the wine was prepared it was usually put away in the spare room upstairs, next to the warmth of the central chimney. There it would ferment, and when it had 'worked off' it would be bottled, with the intention of 'saving some for Christmas'. This early preparation for the festive season was necessary as most families could expect large numbers of visitors, especially during the 'Twelve Days of Christmas', a special highlight of the year which was celebrated accordingly.

Many folk would point out that alcohol "has its own place, all the same." Outside of the day to day work situation, it is all the more appreciated in its appropriate social setting—the ceilidh or family celebration. But without any doubt the prevalent drink is a 'good cup of tea'. Domestic traditions may have undergone many changes over the years, but the welcome of the Codroy Valley kitchen, the heart of the home, has always remained constant. There, in the warmth of hospitality, the visitor is made welcome, and the kettle immediately brought to the boil, regardless of how busy the housewife may be.

CHAPTER 5

The Twelve Days of Christmas

We wouldn't miss a night!
Margaret Cormier (née MacArthur]

U ntil as recently as the 1960s, there was one time of the year, the Twelve Days of Christmas, which stood out as being especially memorable for the Codroy Valley people who celebrated the festivities in the 'old-time' way. During the Twelve Days, which in the Valley ran from Christmas Day, December 25, to Old Christmas Day, January 6,[1] they had more ceilidhs than at any other period of the year.

There was much to get ready for the Christmas season and the preparations began well in advance, when everyone looked forward with eager anticipation to the highlight of their long winter. Although there was so much work to be done, Allan and Mary MacArthur's daughter Margaret (Mrs. Leo Cormier), said that everyone "used to love for Christmas to come, for it was all fun and frolic."

While the term 'the Twelve Days of Christmas' could still be heard in the Valley until well into the 1960s, the actual activities involved in the celebrations were modified as the years went by, until finally there were no longer any Twelve Days set aside to be observed in the traditional manner. Consequently, some of the description here is only applicable to the very early years in the area, and much of it typifies what went on during the last forty years.

Although he did not provide the bulk of the information for this chapter, it was Allan MacArthur himself who initiated the interest in the topic. On one of the first days of January 1970, Allan was seated in his own chair surrounded by his family and friends, enjoying the warmth of a winter fire. As we all welcomed in the New Year that marked the beginning of another decade, Allan showed obvious pleasure that his old homestead, the gathering place of family and friends since the turn of the century, could still be the centre of a real ceilidh. There was still a considerable amount of Gaelic spoken by most of the people there, with more than enough English added to make sure that no one was left out of the conversation. The afternoon was filled with many things which characterized an old-time ceilidh which could have been held during the Twelve Days of Christmas that the old people once knew.

Allan, the centre of almost all the activities, steered the conversation along its various channels, prompted the songs from his visitors and suggested the pipe music. It came to him naturally and without effort to include all his company in the activities of the ceilidh, and he invariably knew the potential of each person to contribute his or her talent to the conversation, songs, and music, and balanced that with contributions of his own in the different areas of interest. During the course of the afternoon, I noted Allan's special interest in comparing his memories of the old way of celebrating the Christmas season to my mother's recollections of the old days on the Isle of Skye. Although I had spent my childhood on that same island, I had known nothing of this aspect of life there until I heard the discussion between my mother and Allan MacArthur.

Over the span of five years following this memorable occasion, I was given further details of the Twelve Days of Christmas during a series of other visits with the MacArthur family. In all, four members of the family from three generations described their recollections of the Twelve Days, and it was interesting to notice the different points of view they took on the separate occasions when they gave their accounts.

Mrs. MacArthur provided much of the information on the preparation for the festive season and on the role of the women in general. From her report, the preparation sounded as if it were not out of the ordinary but her daughter, Margaret, confirmed my suspicions of her mother's modesty as she remembered how much hard work was so willingly undertaken by her mother and grandmother, and women in general, to make the Christmas season a success. Margaret also added a considerable amount of information, filling in the gaps when her parents were no longer there for me to rely upon. While she recalled many of the details, I was able to observe yet another facet of tradition-bearing in the Codroy Valley when some of her own eight children, then ranging in ages from ten to twenty-one, became interested in hearing their mother talk of days gone by. The rest of the details came to me from Angus MacNeill, grandson of Allan MacArthur, who was born in the early 1940s. Viewed from their separate generations, each gave accounts which concentrated on different aspects, with all four complementing each other.

As already mentioned, preparation for the Christmas toast began around September. Mrs. MacArthur recalled that they got ready well in advance of the season when a keg or two of wine or beer, or both, were put aside by most families after the autumn berry-picking. There were also a few men in days gone by who prepared moonshine specially for the Christmas season. The women baked cakes in October and November, usually one or two large dark fruit cakes and a light fruit cake, and put them away (sometimes wrapped in muslin soaked in rum to add to the flavour and texture) in air-tight containers to mature for Christmas. Other baking was done as well, but they would usually wait until much closer to Christmas before baking shortbread and additional treats. In the autumn, when all the housewives were busy bottling fruit, vegetables and meat for the winter, they took into account when calculating the amounts to bottle that they would need a substantial amount to set aside for the Twelve Days alone, when they could expect to feed many extra visitors during the days of the festivities.

The food, however, was only a part of all the preparations, for there were many other tasks to be accomplished before Christmas Eve arrived. During the autumn evenings when the children were in bed, the women busied themselves knitting, sewing, or crocheting items of clothing to be given as Christmas gifts to various members of the family. Margaret recalled that no matter what else they got for Christmas as children, they always got socks their mother had knitted. Mrs. MacArthur considered them to be special Christmas socks, and rather than make them the standard grey colour, she dyed them shades of bright green or red: "More than once Mom used to be up late, dyeing our socks, a couple of nights before Christmas."

As Christmas Eve drew closer, the women were especially busy cleaning the house and putting everything in order, for it was very important that nothing be out of place or in need of cleaning, tidying, or mending during the Christmas season. As a result the women, already busy, as a rule found themselves working harder than ever to make sure that the Twelve Days could be spent attending only to the activities of the season without unnecessary housecleaning or mending to interfere with all the socializing that went on. This did not mean, however, that the women finally found time to sit back and rest; they directed their energy toward the additional preparation and cooking of meals and catering to visitors, rather than toward their usual everyday tasks.

As Christmas approached and most of the larger housecleaning jobs were completed, the family turned their attention to decorating their home for the festive season. In the earlier days the only decoration they knew was the greenery of the spruce, fir, holly, or some other evergreen twigs and branches, which they twined around the doorposts and window frames on the outside of the house and around the larger picture frames on the inside. This age-old custom of decorating houses with greenery goes back to time immemorial, and was standard throughout many parts of the world before the German idea of the Christmas tree was adopted during the reign of Queen Victoria.

Not long after her marriage to Allan MacArthur in 1923, Mrs. MacArthur decided she would try having a Christmas tree in her home decorated for the occasion, an idea novel to the Codroy Valley. Although she did not mention it herself, Margaret told me that her mother was the first person in the Valley ever to have a Christmas tree. When her neighbours saw her taking the tree into the house, they all wondered "what in the world she was doing!" Margaret did not know where her mother had heard of the idea, already popular in other parts of America, but it possibly may have been from her husband who told her of the year (1910) when he worked in a nursery which shipped Christmas trees from Maine to other parts of the United States. Allan may also have described to her how he had seen the trees decorated while he was in the 'Boston States' or in Nova Scotia. Whatever the source, the new idea soon caught on, and from the 1920s onward it has been the custom throughout the Valley to have a Christmas tree each year (*right*).

A few days before Christmas Eve all the children of the family old enough to walk in the woods would set off with their father or an older brother to choose the Christmas tree. There was always a great feeling of excitement about this event which, for the children, marked the beginning of their involvement in the Christmas season. Having made their choice of a well-shaped tree, usually a fir, they would chop it down and drag it home through the snow; or, if they were fortunate enough to have been taken out by the horse and sleigh, they would tie their tree on to the sleigh, jump aboard, and head for home. There they would brush the snow off the tree and leave it outside the house for a few days before carrying their prize into 'the room' on Christmas Eve.

After the Christmas tree was safely anchored in a bucket of sand, the children would set to work decorating it. By today's standards decorations were none too elaborate, simply a few homemade ornaments of coloured paper, with fluffs of raw sheep's wool to simulate snow. As the years went by, however, and commercially-made decorations became available, they moved along with the times toward today's lavishly-decorated trees that are part of almost all North American homes at Christmas.

In the meantime, while the children decorated the tree in the room, their mother and perhaps the oldest girls in the family would be in the kitchen baking a few last minute cookies and pies and making the final preparations for the family Christmas dinner to be cooked the next day. Margaret recalled many Christmas Eves when her job was to ice the cakes her mother had made.

Mary and Allan MacArthur, Christmas c.1955.

On Christmas Eve the very young children were put to bed and were usually looked after by their grandmother, who would stay in the house while the family would wrap up warmly in their winter clothing, about eleven o'clock at night, all ready to attend Midnight Mass in their local church. When the horse was harnessed and a rug or old blanket put on top of the sleigh, the members of the family would all climb aboard and, with a feeling of excitement and anticipation of the pleasure they looked forward to during the Twelve Days, would set off in the crisp winter air to the parish church. They usually tried to get there at least a quarter of an hour earlier than Mass began, for they knew the church would be packed, and a large family would have little chance of sitting together if they arrived at the last minute. Normally, this would not seem important, but since Christmas was a time of family unity and reunions, they liked to begin all together on the very first celebration of the season, Midnight Mass.

After Mass was over, a great atmosphere of excitement would prevail outside the church as they stopped to wish relatives and friends "Nollaig Chridheil," "Merry Christmas" or "Joyeux Noel." Generally they did not wait outside the church for very long, partly because the winter nights were cold, but mostly because they were anxious to get the family back home to greet the person who had 'kept house' and to begin their own family celebration.

Upon arriving at their home and after taking off their outdoor clothing, the family would gather in 'the room', where they completed their Christmas wishes. The younger children who had been allowed to go to Mass, and who were probably very tired by this time, were given a glass of milk, a piece of *bonnach*,[2] and a goodnight kiss, then sent to bed with the excited reminder that Santa Clause would be coming. Afterwards the rest of the family would sit around the kitchen table which had been set while they were at Mass. Usually, this meal consisted of cold meats prepared earlier in the day, some home-bottled pickles, home-baked bread, *bonnach*, and the first of their Christmas cakes, along with a cup of 'good strong tea'. When the kitchen chores were finished, all those who had not gone to bed sat in 'the room' and enjoyed a few drinks to wish each other good health. In some families the adults exchanged their gifts or opened any that awaited them at this time.

In the early days, and right up until the late 1940s, Santa Claus did not generally have the task of filling stockings in the Codroy Valley, for the children there had never heard of such a thing. Margaret recalled that she hadn't seen a stocking hung up during her childhood, and it was not until after her own first child was born in the early 1950s that she became familiar with the custom which, by that time, had been introduced to the Valley. Not that Santa neglected the children but, as Margaret said, "He used to leave each child a package under the Christmas tree which would usually contain an apple, some candy, a pair of socks, and sometimes other clothing, and one little toy." While Margaret's own children were astonished at the contentment of their mother's generation with the seemingly meagre gains from Christmas—after all, children nowadays can have candies, apples, and clothing any day of the year, and small toys are only small rewards—their mother assured them that they used to get as much or more pleasure out of their little Christmas package as children today get out of their annual 'haul'. She recalled with amusement one Christmas when her uncle asked her brother, Martin, what Santa had left for him; quick as a flash came the eager reply: "Candy, ubhal, stocainnean, agus reithe beag." [Candy, an apple, socks, and a little ram.][3] Although she had no idea where her parents had obtained Martin's little toy ram, Margaret did know that he was more than delighted with it.

During the earlier days the gifts exchanged by their parents were by no means elaborate. Typical 'adult gifts' were fancy handkerchiefs for the women, socks and ties for the men. Margaret emphasized that the gifts were not their main enjoyment of Christmas, but it was 'all the fun and frolic' they had during the Twelve Days of Christmas that they looked forward to the most. Her children seemed rather dismayed they had never had the privilege of participating in a Christmas such as their mother knew, or even their older cousins whose ages were mid-way between their generation and their mother's. For example, Angus MacNeill, Margaret's nephew who was born when she was in her teens, had Christmas memories which were closer to Margaret's than to those of his younger cousins whom he regarded as a new generation. Angus's recollections of Christmas did not compare in any way to descriptions from today's children who place almost all the emphasis on the gifts. His was rather the excitement of being part of the adult celebration. While he mentioned the gifts only in passing, he said nothing of the Christmas dinner his grandmother once described: the family would kill and roast a couple of hens or a big rooster or have a big roast of pork, along with all their own vegetables, followed by a 'Washington Pie' which was two sponge cakes with home-bottled raspberries in between the layers and whipped cream on the top. Christmas dinner, though today not identical to what it was in the days when they produced the ingredients in the Valley, would always be with them. What Angus regretted was that their way of celebrating the Christmas season, with all its tradition and excitement, had changed so drastically from what the old people had once known, and from what he had seen during his own childhood.

It was very late one night during his grandmother's wake in January of 1975 that Angus sat by the kitchen table where they had always gathered as children. He remembered the days when the home of his MacArthur grandparents was the centre of their family traditions, where Gaelic was spoken all the time. There they loved to gather with family and friends, especially during the Twelve Days of Christmas. As he sat there telling me the things he remembered from his childhood during the 1940s, he reminded me that I "should be taking note of all these old things now that the old folk are gone," and reassured by the fact that I took a pencil and a scrap of paper, he and one of his contemporaries reminisced and laughed together, relating the pranks they played at school, the pranks other people were said to have played at wakes and weddings, and the fun they used to have during the festive season. As Angus spoke, I jotted down as much as I could, as fast as I could, and as far as possible I have tried to write his account as he told it:

They used to celebrate the Twelve Days of Christmas here at one time. I remember when we were children, they would arrange to have a big 'time' [party] in a different house every night during the Twelve Days of Christmas, and usually they'd have the first night here at Grandpa's [Allan MacArthur's] house. They [the adults who were attending] would harness the horse and sleigh, and then the whole family would set off for the 'time'. When they would get to the house they would put all the children up in the bedrooms, which were pretty cool, and they were told to go to sleep there while the parents went downstairs to enjoy the party. Before they would settle down to that, the men would unharness the horses, take them up beside the barn, and there they would tether them, each one covered with a blanket, and the ten or fifteen horses standing right close to one another to help keep them warm.

Then there would be the biggest kind of a time with Grandpa playing the pipes, and people singing and playing the accordion and the fiddle, and with dancing and step-dancing. And of course there would be plenty to eat; the women would make a big 'feed' with bottled meats and pickles and jams, bannocks, breads, pies, and Christmas fruit cakes, and when they'd get hungry part of the way through, they'd have a cup of tea and a feed. And of course there would be lots to drink all through, with whisky and rum and lots of home-brew. Then after they drank two or three gallons of home-brew, they would wake up the children, carry them down in their blankets, and put them on the sleigh to take them home. Now, you'd be right sleepy, probably at three or four o'clock in the morning, and they'd take you out and put you on that sleigh, and by the time they'd harness up the horse again, and they'd be laughing and feeling good, and you'd be freezing to death, trying to sit closer together to keep warm!

They didn't think anything of taking us out like that in those days, but nowadays if you let one of the kids outside the door for a minute and he hasn't been all done up in a snowsuit and cap and mitts to keep out the cold, the old people are there telling you that you're letting the poor child freeze to death! Yes, they used to have some times in them days, every night during the Twelve Days of Christmas.

Throughout the season people usually attempted to visit all their family and friends in their own and neighbouring communities in the Valley. While an afternoon ceilidh or an evening of merriment such as Angus described probably would have taken care of all the visiting they wished to do, there was yet another type of visit peculiar to the Christmas season of earlier days. From Christmas Night to Old Christmas Night householders could, on any evening after dusk, anticipate a few visits from local mummers—people dressed up in some disguise with a mask on, who visited various homes in their neighbourhood for fun and excitement and to enjoy the various activities of the evening. No advance notice of the visit was given to any particular house, and the more unexpected the visit, the more fun the mummers got from it.

Margaret remembered that during the years when mummering was an annual custom in most homes, "all during Christmas there was a bunch of old clothes and things kept aside for mummering." In her own family, Allan and Mary MacArthur kept the clothes in a big barrel in the back porch so that whoever decided to go out mummering could delve into the ready supply; and if they so wished, they could wear a different 'rig' every night. Margaret added that during her teens and early twenties she and her brothers "didn't miss a night going out mummering."

The mummering neither preceded nor followed the arranged ceilidhs that were held all during the Twelve Days, but it was cleverly interwoven with them. One could accept an invitation to a ceilidh and go mummering at the same house on the same evening, provided some ingenuity was used to fool the host. In fact, Margaret recalled schemes in which she was involved where she actually went mummering at her own house with a friend, without anyone initially suspecting it. Choosing a moment when the evening's activities were in full swing with the house crowded with family and friends, she and a friend "skipped upstairs unnoticed, changed into some foolish rigs, put on masks, and sneaked out of the [seldom used] front door at the foot of the stairs, while everyone was so busy having a grand time out in the kitchen." They went round to the back door where all visitors familiar with the area would have entered and, rapping loudly on the door, they entered the house without anyone knowing who they were or where they had come from. Eventually, after much guessing and 'fooling around', someone guessed who they were and "everyone had a grand joke all round." The entire idea of Christmas in those days was to get as much fun out of, and put as much fun into, the Twelve Days of Christmas as they possibly could.

Mummers usually visited in small groups. Margaret recalled a typically good night of mummering when she, two of her brothers—Sears and George—and her cousin took the horse and sleigh and visited almost every house from their own home on the Grand Codroy River all the way over to St. Andrews on the Little Codroy River, and completed the loop of road via Loch Lomond until they were back home. They dressed that evening in "homemade rigs of brin bags [hemp sacks]" and hardly a soul recognized them. Although mummers would sometimes make 'rigs' such as Margaret described, they almost always dressed in whatever was available in the way of old or eccentric clothing—old, worn pants [trousers], long underwear, old-fashioned or torn dresses, strange footwear, such as long rubber hip-waders, old hats, or whatever else they could find. Much of the fun of mummering was in getting dressed up and laughing at the unlikely costumes of the others in the party, as some men dressed as women and vice versa. Margaret added that "mind you, one of these long, old-fashioned dresses didn't feel so good when you'd be walking through the snow with the bottom of it wet on the last of it!" One of Margaret's children remembered that sometimes the mummers would carry an old gun, or even a broom pretending it was a gun, which though in fun sometimes frightened the children.

The masks worn by the mummers were always homemade however and "there was no such a thing as masks you could buy." They were constructed from a variety of materials, such as an old flour bag with two holes cut out for eyes, with black crayon or ink around them, and a hole for the mouth emphasized by lipstick. Sometimes similar masks were made from a strong paper bag or a cardboard box, and pieces of rags attached to the back to look like raggedy hair hanging down.

In his article, "The Mask of Friendship: Mummering as a Ritual of Social Relations,"[4] John F. Szwed discussed the custom of Christmas mummering in the Newfoundland community of 'Ross', his pseudonym for a typical settlement or 'section' of the Codroy Valley. He describes the mummers entering the house and their subsequent actions:

Uninvited, they enter the house noisily without knocking, stamping their feet heavily as they approach the door as they pass into the kitchen. Once inside, they begin a jogging, half-dance, half-shake that is the 'mummer's walk'. They often move about the room freely and will sometimes go into other parts of the house; they are aggressive and may nudge or jostle members of the household or begin dancing with them or other mummers. They may make jokes about the family. Frequently, the mummers bring musical instruments and may play guitars or violins, or beat on bread pans. One or two mummers might step-dance if asked to do so.

I was a little puzzled by Szwed's remarks about musical instruments since this seemed to indicate to me the possibility of a complete give-away of the identity of any mummer who might have been one of the Valley's more accomplished musicians—and there were nine MacArthurs who immediately came to mind! I decided to ask Margaret to comment on the paragraph quoted above, and on three others I had selected from the same article. Without knowing that 'Ross' was the pseudonym for her own Codroy Valley, she took the paragraphs and, with attention to detail I had previously thought was only characteristic of her father, went through them phrase by phrase, making careful comments as she went. Where possible, I have tried to use her own words which I wrote down as she spoke.

It was true, she said, that they were not invited, as the surprise was part of the fun, but they always knocked loudly on the door before walking in. Usually they did not wait for someone to answer the door, but the loud knocks gave a moment's warning that the mummers were at their house. Yes, they stamped their feet, Margaret said, and when she read Szwed's description of the 'mummers walk' she laughed heartily and said that was just what they did, but without showing it she, herself, would find that difficult to put into words. She also agreed that they went out of the kitchen, usually into the sitting room if they thought someone was missing out on their visit, and there were times when they'd "have a bit of fun" and nudge someone, but she did not equate this behaviour with aggression as Szwed did. She said that it was only playful and that no one minded, especially as they all had "real fun when the mummers danced with each other or with the people in the house." When she came to the part where Szwed mentioned that the mummers made jokes about the family, she laughed and said she'd never forget one year when a bunch of mummers came to her own house when her children were very young. She had a new baby in the crib in the kitchen, and one of the mummers looked in and remarked to everyone, "Oh, my gosh, don't he look like P—!" This type of joke would no doubt have been uproariously funny to everyone, even if it did come as a surprise to Margaret, since this man in question was an old bachelor who lived alone.

When she came to the section where Szwed referred to mummers playing musical instruments, Margaret said that this was true, but generally they would only play the mouth organ which they could do underneath their masks. In the Codroy Valley the mouth organ was not one of the more common instruments played at a party, and although "anyone who plays music can play one," they were generally played by children or taken to sporting cabins in the country where anything larger was too bulky to carry. Margaret could not recall mummering with anyone who played any of the other instruments: "My good gosh, if Sears, or Leonard or Uncle Johnny, or Jimmie, or any of those played, people would know right away who they were, and what good would there be in that?" She said that they would step-dance, however, and even her brother Frank, who was known all over the Valley for his superb dancing, would "do a few foolish steps, but none of his own" to see if he'd fool them all the more. She also added to the description by saying that whenever they spoke they would use 'mummer's talk', which was done in a high-pitched tone, while inhaling, in very rapid speech. One of her children remembered a time when their Uncle Sears MacArthur, one of Margaret's younger brothers, went mummering at the house and revealed to them afterwards that he had put a button under his tongue to disguise his voice.

In a later part of his article, Szwed mentioned that it was no fun if the mummers were identified too soon, and no fun if they were not recognized at all. Margaret agreed with the first point but qualified it by saying that "if you walk in and someone said your name right soon, you wouldn't feel like doing anything; you'd just stay right quiet." She was of the opinion, however, that it was all the more fun if no one recognized the mummers at all, as they would have a grand time among themselves all the way to the next house, joking about how they "fooled them" and speculating as to what the conversation might be among the people they'd just left, or planning what they would say or hint to them next time they saw them.

From the moment the mummers entered the house, the people there would try to identify them, and as the mummers played their roles, frolicking and taking the liberties allowed to mummers, their hosts would ask them questions and carefully study their mannerisms whenever they could. Some of the old people were especially good at recognizing the hands of their friends and occasionally, if a mummer came to the house with gloves on, there were a few people who could overcome even that disguise. Margaret recalled her father in particular who, if he still did not know who the mummers were after a multitude of questions, would casually ask: "Can you play crib?" Generally they would, like most Codroy Valley people, be card game enthusiasts and on receiving an affirmative reply, Allan MacArthur would say, "Very well, then, let's have a game." Margaret said her father, who "pretty well played with everyone he knew at one time or another," would know almost right away who they were by the way they played cards. She illustrated her point by recalling one year before she was married when "this mummer came to the house alone. Now, that was kind of funny anyhow because you wouldn't usually go alone." She described how all the family were puzzled as to who he was. He was "dressed in the funniest rig," and they just could not figure him out. "By and by, Dad asked him if he could play crib; and as soon as he saw him put out his hand of crib, Dad knew right away because of the way he held the cards in his left hand!" The mystery caller turned out to be none other than Leo Cormier, the man Margaret married some time later!

Once identified, the mummer unmasked and returned to the normal role of a visitor, when he was offered food and something to drink (*page 114*). Usually, they were given a piece of Christmas cake or something baked, and as Margaret said, "There were times when you'd have walked a good long way, and you'd be pretty darned glad of something to eat." If they planned on visiting several other houses, the mummers generally stayed only a short time, perhaps ten minutes after they had eaten; but if they were at the last house on their itinerary then they would stay for a ceilidh with the family as non-mummering guests.

Probably the most controversial part of Szwed's article is his remark:

> But perhaps more important to the mummer is the aggression which he can freely express towards his host, and yet be protected from the usual reprisals while he is in this "other worldy" or [in Durkheim's terms] "sacred state."[5]

I asked Margaret for a comment upon this final statement. She was most surprised that any mummers would go out mummering so that they could show aggression towards their host, as she emphasized that they would only go to the houses where they "knew the people real well, or if someone you were with knew them." She wondered how anyone who did that could live in the place afterwards, and, convinced that it certainly would not have been possible in the Codroy Valley said, "My gosh, I can't go along with that—certainly not to my knowledge, and God knows we did enough of it! I wonder where is he talking about anyway?"

The mummers unmasked: Mary MacDonald (later Mrs. Allan MacArthur) with a friend. The girls were dressed as men—and smoking! (1920s).

The Twelve Days of Christmas were certainly filled with "fun and frolic" as Margaret said: "We wouldn't miss a night. We'd walk, and walk, and walk, and come home all hours in the night, tired out." Yet, full of energy, they were all set to go again the next night. Although Allan MacArthur himself had been a mummer over many years, as his daughter pointed out, in his old age his main interest was the comparison of the Gaelic oral tradition connected with the festive season and the ceilidhs that would take place during it.

One particular night during the Twelve Days of Christmas, set apart from all others and recognized by Scotsmen the world over, is New Year's Eve. Allan MacArthur did not, however, refer to this night by the Lowland term 'Hogmanay' which in recent years has even been adopted by Highlanders. Even when speaking English, Allan used the name *Oidhche Challuinn* which his forebears brought over from Scotland, along with the customs they continued to celebrate in the New World more than a century later.

Allan was in his element reminiscing about the old days when he recalled the "Rann na Calluinn" [the rhyme said on Oidhche Challuinn] which was said at every house visited:

I'll say one in Gaelic, about when we'd be going round the houses beating out the Old Year and taking in the New Year. And then we'd get a big jig of rum when we'd [say]:

Oidhche chullainn Challuinn chruaidh
Thàinig mise le m' dhuan gu taigh.
Thubhairt am bodach rium le gruaim
Buailidh mi do chluais le preas.
Labhair a' chailleach a b'fhearr na'n t-òr
Gum bu chòir mo leigeil a staigh
Air son na dh'ithinn-sa de bhiadh
Agus deuran beag sìos leis.[6]

That was in the old times.

[On a cold frosty Night of the Calluinn
(New Year's Eve)
I came with my rhyme to a house.
The old man said to me with a frown
I'll hit you on the ear with a briar.
Said the old woman who was better that gold
That I should be let in
For all the little food that I would eat
And a little drink to go with it.]

This custom was immediately familiar to my mother, who remembered seeing adults dressed in strange clothes at *Oidhche Challuinn* arriving at the house during her own early childhood in the mid-1920s. She had not seen it since, however, nor heard the *Rann na Calluinn* in its original context. Allan's Codroy Valley rhyme was not identical to the one my mother had heard, although the theme of it—basically the request for entry into the house and for food and drink—was the same. There are many printed texts which cite examples of *Rann na Calluinn*[6] and also several versions recorded orally from the Isles of Skye and Lewis. I have not, however, come across any that are identical to that given by Allan MacArthur. The many examples show an individuality peculiar to each, indicating that the Rann differed from area to area, but all incorporated the theme already mentioned.

The disguises worn in the Valley on Oidhche Challuinn were much the same as one might expect to see on any of the Twelve Days of Christmas. The original attire of Oidhche Challuinn both in Scotland and Cape Breton is reported to have been sheepskins or cowhides and, according to several written descriptions from both countries, they followed the ritual of circling the house sunwise according to the ancient Celtic orientation of all things following the path of the sun.[7]

Allan described Oidhche Challuinn as he remembered it from the days when he and his family and friends dressed up and went out to bring in the New Year:

> The women and the men and the boys, they'd get together and after supper when it would get dark they would club together now... like if there were three or four or five from this house, well they would prepare and go to the next house. And when they'd get to the next house, they would start at the door and go right around the house and every one with a little stick in his hand, you know, beating the house. They was driving out the Old Year and letting the New Year in. And it was all Gaelic, you see. And every door they would come to, well when they'd go around the house they would knock on the door, and the woman would be there and she wouldn't let you in if you didn't have a rhyme, or sing. And when you'd go through with the rhyme, you'd come in and they'd offer you a drink of rum or a drink of whisky or something. And then the crowd in that house would get ready and go to the next house. Well, when they'd be crowd enough of boys and girls, and old men with them too, for to dance, well that's where they would stay. And they would put up a dance, you know, and they wouldn't be short of whisky or rum either. Well that's the way they used to spend New Year's Night [Eve], you know, probably seventy years ago, or something like that.

Just as the Gaelic language gradually faded from everyday use, so too the *Rann na Calluinn* was forgotten by all but the very old, until eventually the custom disappeared altogether and the Twelve Days of Christmas became a thing of the past, memories to be described to children who knew nothing of this kind of Christmas. Allan MacArthur regretted that "it died out here, and it turned to something else," and his daughter, Margaret, told her children "In those days, we just used to hate to see Christmas ending. Today, it's just a money racket, and everyone is glad when it's over now." With a few childhood memories of seeing mummers coming into their homes during the last few years that the customs survived, along with their mother's description of the Christmas seasons of her youth, even the younger children today show some regret that they are no longer likely to have any part of the traditions of the Twelve Days of Christmas—traditions their forebears kept for over a century in the Codroy Valley.

CHAPTER 6

Traditional Oral Narrative

> We used to have a lot of that in Gaelic, but
> none in English.
> *Allan MacArthur, 1970*

For centuries the people of the Highlands and Islands of Scotland have been known to have a great interest in tales and legends about many different topics, ranging from the ordinary to the supernatural. The old people especially remember the long winter evenings spent telling stories that had been handed down through generations.

It was only natural, then, that this custom was carried over to the New World with the migrations of the eighteenth and nineteenth centuries. It was certainly very much a part of the way of life of the Codroy Valley Scots, whom Allan MacArthur clearly recalled telling stories, and passing on the traditions that they had heard from the generations that had gone before. Once a vibrant tradition, storytelling was the one feature of the ceilidh which suffered most from the changes in the way of life that had taken place over the past few decades. Unfortunately, the decline was apparent by the time I first visited the area for, in spite of the fact that Allan MacArthur was once a main part of this tradition, he felt it had faded to such an extent that the context in which the stories were once told, with the atmosphere they created, were more alive in his memory than the stories themselves. He emphasized that the old language, Gaelic, was at the very heart of this tradition.

The stories themselves were not kept for an exclusive 'narrative session' but were usually interwoven with songs, or quite simply with the day's news. They fitted well into the general interest and entertainment of the ceilidh.

The stories collected here are mostly legend and were recalled in a setting which was, for Allan MacArthur, nothing like the original story-telling situation. He retold them on quiet visits during warm summer afternoons—not only were they told 'out of season' but the atmosphere and the entire situation could not come close to the real storytelling setting Allan grew up with. In the old days, after all, most storytelling took place on winter evenings, when early nightfall made outside work impossible.

On those afternoons when Allan told a few stories, his audiences were usually made up of his wife, my mother and me, and occasionally a few of his old friends who called to see him, since they also had left their farm work to younger, more able members of their families. I cannot understate the importance of having my mother with me during these particular recording sessions; she unconsciously provided Allan with a very real link with the Old Country and the customs which he associated with his Gaelic-speaking compatriots. As a child my mother had attended the same kinds of ceilidh that interested Allan MacArthur, for her own parents' home in the community of Glenconon, Isle of Skye, was a popular ceilidh house. She was well acquainted with the comings and goings of the winter evenings and there, or at a neighbouring ceilidh house, she loved to listen to the old men or to her father relate the long histories, legends and tales. The children were expected to remain silent, and for long hours did so, happily engrossed in all that went on at such a ceilidh. The same code of behaviour was also expected of the Codroy Valley children, and to a certain extent this has survived even in today's child-oriented societies. Comparisons between the two traditions were numerous, and Allan MacArthur (the expert interviewer) was obviously in his element as he questioned my mother and prompted her to tell him of the days of her childhood. He had the ability to elicit detail, and was delighted to hear of times when the host of some of the ceilidhs she attended would show attention to the children present by giving each one a penny, along with directions on how to make it shine like new by polishing it for a long time with the ashes from one of the men's tobacco pipes—perhaps an attempt to divert the younger minds from the topics being discussed by the adults. She and Allan laughed together as they recalled the times they left the fireside of a neighbour's home, terrified to venture out in the dark, lest a ghost, witch, or 'each uisge' [water horse] would get them on the way home. Throughout most of his life Allan had also experienced the thrill of sitting in the company of good storytellers, intently listening to every detail, imagining the things they described, and being transported to the world of travellers, pirates, ghosts, witches, and other supernatural beings. Despite the fact that my mother was unable to relate the stories she had heard so often, the reality of the situation in which they were told was of equal importance to Allan MacArthur.

On afternoons such as these, Allan would relate the history and long-forgotten aspects of rural and domestic life, and recall old songs of many verses. His extraordinarily clear memory would immediately impress his listeners, and many of them would remark upon this fact. He himself, however, would often apologize if he could not provide some detail he wanted to include; he would feel let down that he was "after forgetting" and sometimes would shake his head and say that he was "after getting too old to remember." Nevertheless, there still remained considerable material from the entire body of narrative with which he was once familiar.

In the homes of the Scottish settlers, the storytelling was always in the mother tongue: "We used to have a lot of that in Gaelic but none in English." They had several kinds of narrative, but Allan MacArthur was of the opinion that the most popular were the historical kind:

> Well, the old people here, especially the Scots, you know, they would gather together, well it would be always stories about Scotland, you know, the place they left and how hard it was for them when they left Scotland...came out to America— Canada, and Newfoundland especially—what a hard time they had to get along. And some of them, you see, they were sorry for leaving Scotland, for although they thought it was so hard in Scotland, they found that it was worse out in America, a lot worse.

Some of the historical legends about Scotland and the times emigration took place have already been dealt with in Chapter 2. This chapter will cover the remaining types of narrative told by Allan MacArthur. For the purposes of presentation, I have divided the stories into groups and shall precede each one with a suitable title, even though Allan himself did not assign titles to them.

Adventure

In the early days, piracy was a topic around which several stories were told "because Newfoundland was full of pirates at one time." The pirates plundered many ships around the coastal waters, and it was said that they sometimes buried money obtained in their escapades:

120

They buried the money around Newfoundland in places, and over around Cape Breton too, and Nova Scotia and those places. But Newfoundland used to be such a wonderful place for pirates but not so much as Nova Scotia and those places, because they'd have come so far, you see, Spain, and from places like that.

It was also said there were people who had found pirate money:

But you'd never find out. If they got pirate money you'd never find out.... Well, I don't know why... they had that kind of a way, you see. Well, another thing, their word was their oath, you see; not so today—the word is no good today. You can't depend on a person telling you anything. But at that time if they'd find out you were telling lies they had no more use for you.

Piracy was not, however, confined to the seas around North America. From the very area in Scotland which was the home of some of Allan's forebears, there are several exciting accounts of pirates preserved by the Reverend Charles MacDonald in his book *Moidart; or Among the Clanranalds.*

Allan also recalled hearing stories about people who had dreams of finding treasure, but best-remembered was this pirate legend:

The Pirate Ship

In the Gut O' Canso, there was one time a pirate ship came in, you know, for shelter. And she stole before that; she plundered a ship and killed all except the bo'sun boy—probably he might have been around fourteen or sixteen. And they kept him with them; he was a wonderful smart boy, and the pirate kept him with him. And they were one time...off the coast on the Nova Scotia side, near the Gut O' Canso where the schooners used to anchor. Anyhow, the pirate came in and he stayed there; they were resting, you see. They were after plundering a few ships, and they had whatever they want, I suppose. And then this little boy (he was belonged to Nova Scotia) he remembered that there was one ship that wasn't far that was anchored not very far from the pirate. And, you know, the tide runs strong in through the Gut O' Canso where it's blocked off there. But anyhow, this fellow...little boy, when they'd be down or below or busy at something, he'd be on deck and he'd be always watching the schooner, you see. And what did he do but he got a bottle and he wrote a note and he tied a string on the bottle, and he let this string out; he put it where they wouldn't see it if they would come on deck. He tied it somewhere, and the string was strong enough so the bottle would go down to the schooner, you see.

And by gosh, it was only there part of a day (it was in the night-time, and late in the evening and early in the morning that he would use this bottle) but they picked it up. However, he told them all about that they were pirates, you know, where he was, and everything else. And by cripes, before the pirate got out, you know, there was...war. And they didn't know what the boy done, but if they had he would have been thrown overboard. But anyhow, they caught 'em and the whole lot of them was killed. Well, that happened in the Gut O' Canso. And this boy, you know, I don't know how much money they gave him because he went about it this way, and he got cleared...he got saved. They demanded him first, the boy.

The Supernatural

At one time in the Codroy Valley it was fairly common to hear accounts of supernatural happenings. Just as in Scotland, people spoke of fairies and witches and ghosts, although one seldom hears of them today. The stories were convincing and many involved firsthand accounts. Remembering the times when people often spoke of ghosts, Allan MacArthur said it was common in the Valley for people to see ghosts, "when there was nothing, only people, no post office, no church, no law, no nothing...but lots of ghosts!" His mother and grandmother often told of incidents which happened in Scotland: "The people in Scotland were full of that sort of story, and it came over with them." And indeed he accurately summed up the very pattern which was familiar to my own family on Skye—we were surrounded by stories of the supernatural.

Several years ago, there appeared ghost lights at a place by the north bank of the Grand Codroy River, known as Gale's Island. These ghost lights appeared after sundown, but no one could explain why. Allan MacArthur described his experience of the lights:

Ghost Lights

Many's a time I watched it.... It was in the same place for years and years. It would stay on the ground for a little while first, then you would see it rising, rising, and it might go up twenty feet. And then it would burst like, and it would shiver again and turn a different colour, you know, kind of red, and come down to the ground again. And it would stay on the ground probably for five minutes, and then when you'd see it moving again, it would start to get up, rising up and getting bright, and getting bigger. It would go so high. But we were so used to it we didn't mind. But then it disappeared after so many years. Perhaps they used to see it for twenty-five years, and then it disappeared altogether.

The Codroy Valley, again like the Highlands and Islands of Scotland, had its legends of the 'wee folk'. It was not, however, until Allan MacArthur knew that I was from a background where fairies were spoken of and often believed in that he abandoned his hesitation of retelling any of the details of them that he had heard from his mother and grandmother. (Who, after all, would wish to put himself in a situation where there was the slightest possibility of being ridiculed for talking about the fairies?) Allan did, however, know several stories of encounters with the fairies, and he was familiar with the characteristics reputed to have been attributed to them.

Mrs. MacArthur introduced the topic by describing them as "little people dressed in green." Her husband then continued:

The Fairies and Changelings

And they used to live in places under the ground. Well, they wasn't natural people, I don't think.... If they would go to a house, you see, and the woman would give them anything, like oatmeal, and whatever dish that they would have, when they would return it there would be a little more in it than what they got.... My mother used to tell us a lot about them. And they used to live kind of underground; I don't think they had houses or anything.... And once a year they would be shifting from one place to another, the lot of them.

Although reputed to be kind beings, the fairies were not to be meddled with. The people seemed to have a sort of respect for them and would do what was considered to be the wishes of the fairies lest they might have any undesirable dealings with them.

Mrs. MacArthur recalled that she had heard the fairies sometimes stole babies from their cradles:

One woman lost her baby, and she went to look in the cradle, there was something else in its place. I believe she brought the baby back after a time, I think.

Mary MacArthur did not know how the baby was brought back. Both she and her husband felt that it was mysterious to them how the fairies behaved:

They say they used to take babies like that, you know, out of the cradle, whatever they used to do with them. Of course, I guess they wouldn't be able to live with them, the fairies, anyway.

It would appear from all accounts that Allan MacArthur's mother often spoke of the fairies to her children. The fear of being stolen by the fairies was a useful threat to keep her children well behaved. Mrs. MacArthur recalled that "She [Allan's mother] used to tell the children to be good or the *sìdhichean* [fairies] would come and steal them." [1] A fear or respect for the fairies was not something only belonging to her children, for Jenny MacArthur demonstrated that she also had consideration for the fairy folk:

> I used to hear my mother saying that when they used to be milking the cows in the cow-yard, that they would spill some over in places so that the fairies could pick it up.

While Allan MacArthur did not say why people spilled milk for the fairies, there is ample evidence that the same thing occurred in Scotland. Donald A. MacKenzie states that offering milk and meal were supposed to appease the fairies, and that when it was spilled on the ground it was supposed to reach them in their subterranean homes. [2]

As far as I could ascertain fairy music, often spoken about in Scotland, was unknown in the Codroy Valley. No one seemed to have heard of fairy musicians or singers, but Allan MacArthur brought to mind one complete story he had heard in his youth about an encounter someone had with the fairies:

The Fairy Lover

It's about a girl... they [the fairies] were shifting anyhow, and there was a girl who happened to see one of them, and she took an awful liking to him; well, they wouldn't be coming back till a year's time, back to where they left, the same place. And this girl, you know, she was giving up the world and everything else. And at last she went to a person that used to advise—they say there was people like that there—what to do, and she told a story about this fairy man, and she wanted some advice what was the best thing to do. He told her that they would be coming back, to remember the day that she seen him with the rest, and in a year's time go in the same place and take an apple with her. Well anyhow, this gave her more courage, you see, and he told her "He'll speak to you."

And he said: "Take an apple, and when you sees him again, split the apple in two, and you hold one half and pass him the other half." Well now, that happened; he looked at her and he spoke to her.... I can't tell the rest [in English], but anyhow he told her that he wasn't belonged to this world, a living person in this world, and he said: "Tha mi fo'n dream uaibhreach a chaidh fhuasgladh a flathanas" thubhairt e. Agus shìn e dhi am pìos ubhal air ais... ["I am of the Proud Ones (fallen angels) who were expelled from Heaven," he said. And he handed her back the piece of apple.]

What was his name? St. Lucifer, was it, that fell out with God? And they say that probably they [the fairies] were some of that tribe, you see. Well, we don't know what happened, if the likes of that ever happened, that they were drove out of Heaven because they were jealous with God, and he [Lucifer] was turned out, and there was a lot of them followed him. Now that's only stories that I heard.... But he gave her to understand that he wasn't of this world naturally, and he passed her the half of the apple back. Of course, it could be true, and it could be only a story. She never got him, and she forgot all about him after that—she was like she was before she ever saw him.

Although the fairy lover theme was fairly common in Scotland, surprisingly MacEdward Leach did not come across it in Nova Scotia. In *Celtic Tales from Cape Breton*, he stated that: "There are, however, few long tales of the fairy and no fairy mistress or lover tales."[3] It is more likely, however, that there were examples, at least in the early days of the Scots in Cape Breton, which Leach unfortunately did not come across while collecting among the Gaelic-speaking people there. More significantly, this only serves to emphasize all the more how Gaelic narratives, such as the few cited here, tended to disappear completely with the decline of the Gaelic language.

The idea of the fairies being fallen angels is one which was widespread all over Scotland, as shown by Alexander Carmichael in *Carmina Gadelica*.[4] There are also many other references to this motif in much of the literature about Scottish narrative and folklore.

Allan MacArthur's actual narration of "The Fairy Lover" confirmed the impression that he was telling his stories in a situation quite different from the one he once knew. He had never heard this, or other stories in English, nor was he himself accustomed to narrating an English version of it. It was, therefore, natural for him to quote the words of the fairy in the language spoken by the fairies he had heard about—Gaelic.

In the same storytelling session, Allan remembered another of his mother's legends, a story about one of the MacCrimmon pipers. Our company that day included Professor Halpert, who was visiting the area. Allan, very much aware of his guest's keen interest and knowledge of Scottish traditions, embarked upon the story. His telling of this legend specially for his English-speaking visitor demonstrates clearly that traditions such as these belong firmly to the language in which they were originally passed on. Allan's struggle to tell it in English was like battling with an enormous magnet and, as will be seen, he was eventually drawn to his mother tongue:

The MacCrimmon Piper

'Se 'n uamh 'se 'n uamh a dh'abras mise ri "tunnel"...well, that means it's dug under the ground. [It's a cave, it's a cave that I call a tunnel....] And they had places like that in Scotland. Well, they used to go a-hide in those places in time of war or if you did a crime or anything and you want to run away. Well, you wouldn't have to do much in Scotland at that time, sure you'd be killed. If you steal, you'd be hung—that was the rule in Scotland one time, for that. If you do any forgery, you'd be hung for that. And they had to have places, you know, proper... àite anns a' mhonadh [places in the moors]—they'd have placen [sic] for to go a-hide. And perhaps they'd be years there before they'd be found.

Well, this is something like this. An uamh, mar tha Uamh Chreang [Uamh Fhraing?[6]]—bha i cho sean Uamh Chreang 's bhiodh na pìobairean, bhiodh na daoine air son fhaighinn a mach dé cho fada chaidh a cladhach bho'n talamh anns an fhuaradh 's cha d'fhuair iad a mach riamh bho'n a thòisich iad air faighinn a mach air 's àireamh nam beothaichean fiadhaich a bhiodh a faighinn ann. Dh'fheuch pìobairean ri faighinn a mach 's bhitheas 'g a marbhadh, na beothaichean a bh'ann bhiodh iad a marbhadh nam piobairean 's dh'fheumadh iad a' phìob a' chumail air falbh cho fad 's a bhiodh an fheodhainn air thalamh gu h-àrd, gun cluinneadh iad a' phìob agus 's e MacCriomain a' fear mu dheireadh a dh'fheuch, agus chaidh esan na b'fhaide na chaidh gin de'n fheodhainn eile, agus rinn e sin, choinnich e na beothaichean a bhiodh a' marbhadh nan daoine, choinnich e pàirt dhiubh sin, 's chuir e port air a' phìob—rinn e fhéin am port. "Cha till MacCriomain, Cha till mi tuilleadh," agus thuig iad, an fheodhainn a bha coiseachd air an talamh, thuig iad am port mu dheireadh—"Nach truagh mi fhéin gun trì lamhan; dà làmh 's a' phìob 's làmh 's a' chlaidheamh.

[Well, this is something like this. The cave, as Uamh Chreang, it was so old Uamh Chreang, and the pipers, the people tried to find out how far into the ground the cave went, but they never did discover this on account of the wild beasts that were there. Some pipers tried to find out, and they were killed; the wild beasts that were there used to kill the pipers, they had to keep the pipes going so that the people above on the ground could hear the pipes, and it was MacCrimmon who was the last one to try, and he went further in than any of the rest, and he did that, he met the beasts that killed the people. He met some of them and played a tune on the pipes—he composed the tune himself "MacCrimmon will not return, I will return no more," and they understood the last tune—"It's a pity that I am without three hands; two hands on the pipes, and one hand on the sword."]

But he couldn't keep the pipes going and kill the animals, you know. And if he had the third hand, you know, he could use the sword, you see, to keep the pipes going. And shortly after that, the pipes faded away. Well, he was killed, you see, and never returned. He was killed, and I think they gave up trying then, because there was a few pipers, you know, lost their lives into it.

The story of a piper exploring a cave inhabited by wild beasts is one which was widespread in Scotland. In the Skye version, the piper is one of the MacCrimmons, hereditary pipers to the MacLeods of Dunvegan. In his book *The Highland Bagpipe*, in which he devoted an entire chapter to the theme of pipers in enchanted caves, W.L. Manson's version from the Isle of Skye closely resembles the legend told by Allan MacArthur.

This particular story is also a fine example of a legend which would have been followed at least by a song, if not by the pipe music also, and the ceilidh that Allan MacArthur knew in his youth was the ideal setting for all three. Unfortunately, by the time I recorded his version of the legend, he had since forgotten the song, and he himself had never played the particular lament on the pipes, even though he remembered his uncle doing so. Quite spontaneously, Allan turned to my mother and asked her to sing "Cumha Mhic Criomain" [MacCrimmon's Lament] which echoes the words of the story in its chorus: "Cha till MacCrioman, Cha till mi tuilleadh" [MacCrimmon will not return, I will not return] is rendered "Cha till, cha till, cha till e tuille" [Return, return, he will not return]. The tape recording of the singing scarcely reflects the old man's contentment or his feeling that his story was "complete."

Witchcraft

At one time it was said that there were witches in the Codroy Valley. The people had a fear of being witched and would at all costs avoid any situation that they thought might lead to such a thing happening. According to Allan, the old people talked about witches, and they believed that some of the Indians who lived in the Valley had the power of witching. Mrs. MacArthur recalled that "there was old squaws here that used to witch people." Her husband added that those Indians who had the power were said to witch people "if you refused them or made them mad or anything." When asked how they did it, he replied:

> Well, there's nobody knows; they'd never tell anybody else, that was a secret among themselves, you see. And some of them had more power to do it than others, that's the way. They were afraid of one another, you know, when it comes to that, 'cos there was some of them they could witch worse than others, you see. All of them couldn't do it, but there was some who could witch you, but not all of them.

Varying circumstances led to people being witched, but it is evident that the Indians did not like to be interfered with:

> Well, if you were in the woods, the white people, if they were in the woods or out close to them when they'd be deer hunting or hunting wild game like that, well they could witch your gun so that your gun could fire but you wouldn't kill nothing, and things like that, you see.

The Indians were also known to have the power to witch animals, as shown by one story told by Allan MacArthur in which he also described some of the features of the way of life of the Indians of the Codroy Valley:

Indians as Witches

Well, I tell you, some of them...well, there wasn't many who could witch you in my time, but now...they used to make baskets, that's what they lived off, making baskets all the time and making butter tubs and things like that. The Indians, they used to live 'long clear of white people and...well, when the trade started around, they used to make baskets and go down to Port aux Basques and sell them. Well, if they'd come across here and they wanted to go to Little River Station we used to call it then [now St. Andrews] with a load of baskets, and they'd want for you to drive them over...well, if you would refuse them they could witch your horse, you see, that probably he'd be cripple for a while, or something like that. Well, that happened here all right, more than once...yes. But according as they were dying out, you know, this was giving out. Well now, today it's no use to mention anything like that, you know; nobody'd believe you that they could do those things.

With the disappearance of the Micmac Indians from the Codroy Valley in the 1930s when those who did not die from tuberculosis moved to Nova Scotia, the apprehension which the other settlers of the Valley felt toward them disappeared also.

Place Lore

Fishermen on the Grand Codroy River, and especially those experienced in guiding sportsmen in the Valley, are usually familiar with all the local placenames. Several guides still tell the legend of how one fishing pool along the river was named after the child of an Indian family who lived there. Although the legend or the naming of the pool have been given no particular date, the incident which brought about the names predates Prowse, who published his *Guide to Newfoundland* in 1895. He has included 'Molly Chiguanay Pool' on his guide map for fishermen on the rivers of the Codroy Valley (page 178). While his spelling is not identical to the usual spelling heard today, it is still the same pool and the location is accurate.

For many years, Allan MacArthur worked at sporting camps with hunters and fishermen, and he had a thorough knowledge of the area and lore about the river. After he spoke of the Indians who once inhabited the Valley, Allan told this legend of how the place in question got its name:

Mollichignic Pool

And a family of them lived out there, and there was one of their children died, and this name they called them Molli or something like that. And she's buried out there somewhere. And they called it Mollichegenic, you know. And then the people came here, they picked up the word and called it Mollichignic; but now they call it Chignic, you see—well they are leaving Molli out. Well... and the way they used to spell it first, it was M-o-l-l-i-c-h-e-g-e-n-i-c. And it was on account of this child that died and was buried up there.... Well, that may be true.

While most of the settlers had little to do with the Micmac Indians, Allan MacArthur was quick to credit them with expertise they had shared with the newcomers. He pointed out that the Indians taught the local people how to spear eels in the Grand Codroy River using a specially made three or four prong fork with barbs on the prongs. Allan was of the opinion that aside from the craft of moccasin-making it was one of the few skills the white settlers learned from the Indians. They did, however, buy their baskets, Allan recalled, in the days when the Micmacs inhabited the area on the north side of the Grand Codroy (near Millville) which, even today, is known as Indian Hill (*see page 43*).

Nursery Tales

With these examples of narrative demonstrating the fact that the storytelling tradition among the Scots of the Codroy Valley was once very strong, I was obliged to leave the collection of folk narrative at this point, gladly accepting the remnants for what Allan said they represented. His children had already told me that they did not know even one short version such as their father had preserved in his memory, and could scarcely remember any of the topics of the tales.

An unexpected occasion arose, however, on the last night of my first summer in the Valley, when Allan and Mary MacArthur decided to hold a ceilidh to bid me farewell. They invited the entire family and sitting in his own chair, surrounded by a wealth of MacArthur talent, Allan quietly presided over the evening of song, music, step-dancing and general conversation. All the family had put in a long day of hard work, the men at harvesting, and the women cooking for their large families and farm helpers besides. The obvious and spontaneous pleasure they derived from this large family gathering was a great source of contentment to the old couple and Allan, much aware of failing health, was heard to comment that he "might not get too many more chances like this, you know." At an uncharacteristically 'early' hour (midnight) he quietly left the company to retire to bed, with no more than a warm smile to his family to signal his departure. His son, Frank, was at that moment playing the accordion for a step-dance, and when he finished the piece he unexpectedly laid down his instrument. With no word of introduction, he affectionately acknowledged his father's exit by reciting a bedtime story that had been their favourite when he and his brothers and sisters were very young.

Murchan is Mearchan

Murchan is Mearchan mar chuala mise roimh iad, chaidh iad 'na choille chnò, 's dhìrich Murchan as a' chraoibh 's mar a leagadh Murchan dh'itheadh Mearchan. Thàinig Murchan a nuas as a' chraoibh, 's dh'fhoighneachd e do Mhearchan

"Dé dhean thu leis mo chuid chnò?"

"Dh'ith mi iad" arsa Mearchan.

"Dé thaghainn a dheanamh ort?"

"Slat a bhuain 's a' choillidh ud shìos, slat a bhuain 's a' choillidh ud shuas 's gabhail air mo thòin."

"C'aìte faigh mi slat?"

Chaidh e far a robh 'n t-slat.

["C'aìte bheil thu dol?" ars' an t-slat.

"Slat a ghabhas air Mearchan 's e 'n déidh mo chnothan ithe."

130

"O chan fhaigh thu mise," ars' an t-slat "gus a faigh thu tuagh a' ghearras mi."

Chaidh e far an robh tuagh.]

"C'àite bheil thu dol?" ars an tuagh.

"Tuagh a ghearras slat a ghabhas air Mearchan, 's e 'n déidh mo chnothan ithe."

"O chan fhaigh thu mise," ars' an tuagh "gus a faigh thu clach a mheileas mi."

Chaidh e far an robh clach.

"C'àite bheil thu dol?" ars' a' clach.

"Clach a'mheileas tuagh, tuagh a' ghearras slat, slat a ghabhas air Mearchan 's e 'n déidh mo chnothan ithe."

"O chan fhaigh thu mise ars' a' chlach, gus a faigh thu uisge fhliuchas mi."

Chaidh e far an robh an t-uisge.

"C'àite bheil thu dol?" ars' an t-uisge.

"Uisge fhliuchas clach, clach a mheileas tuagh, tuagh a ghearras slat, slat a ghabhas air Mearchan 's e 'n déidh mo chnothan ithe."

"O chan fhaigh thu mise," ars' an t-uisge "gus a faigh thu fiadh a shnàmhas mi."

Chaidh e far an robh 'fiadh.

"C'àite bheil thu dol?" ars' am fiadh.

"Fiadh a shnàmhas uisge, uisge fhliuchas clach, clach a mheileas tuagh, tuagh a ghearras slat, slat a ghabhas air Mearchan 's e 'n deidh mo chnothan ithe."

["O chan faigh thu mise" ars' am fiadh "gus am faigh thu gadhar a ruitheas mi."

Chaidh e far an robh gadhar.

" C'àite bheil thu dol?" ars' an gadhar.

"Gadhar a ruithe fiadh, fiadh a shnàmhas uisge, uisge fhliuchas clach, clach a mheileas tuagh, tuagh a ghearras slat, slat a ghabhas air Mearchan 's e 'n déih mo chnothan ithe."

"O chan fhaigh thu mise," ars' an gadhar, "gus am faigh thu ìm a shuathadh... a ghrìosas ri m' chasan.].

Chaidh e far robh 'n t-ìm.

"C'àite bheil thu dol?" ars' an t-ìm.

"Im chasa gadhar, gadhar a ruithe fiadh, fiadh a shnàmhas uisge, uisge fhliuchas clach, clach a mheileas tuagh, tuagh a ghearras slat, slat a ghabhas air Mearchan 's e 'n déidh mo chnothan ithe."

"O chan fhaigh thu mise" ars' an t-im, "gus a faigh thu luch a sgrìobas mi."

Chaidh e far a robh 'lucha.

"C'àite bheil thu dol?" ars' a' lucha.

"Luch a sgrìobas ìm, ìm chasa gadhar, gadhar a ruithe fiadh, fiadh a shnàmhas uisge, uisge fhliuchas clach, clach a mheileas tuagh, tuagh a ghearras slat, slat a ghabhas air Mearchan 's e 'n déidh mo chnothan ithe."

"O chan faigh thu mise" ars' a' lucha gus a faigh thu cat a ruitheas mi."

Chaidh e far an robh an cat.

"C'àite bheil thu dol?" ars' an cat.

"Cat a ruitheas luch, luch a sgrìobas ìm, ìm chasa gadhar, gadhar a ruithe fiadh, fiadh a shnàmhas uisge, uisge fhliuchas clach, clach a mheileas tuagh, tuagh a ghearras slat, slat a ghabhas air Mearchan 's e 'n déidh mo chnothan ithe."

"O chan fhaigh thu mise" ars' an cat "gus a faigh thu deur a bhainne bhon mhart ud thall."

Chaidh e far an robh mart.

"C'àite bheil thu dol?" ars' a' mhart.

"Deuran bhainne bhuat dhan chat, cat a ruitheas luch, luch a sgrìobas ìm, ìm casa gadhar, gadhar a ruithe fiadh, fiadh a shnàmhas uisge, uisge fhliuchas clach, clach a mheileas tuagh, tuagh a ghearras slat, slat a ghabhas air Mearchan 's e 'n déidh mo chnothan ithe."

"O chan fhaigh thu deuran bhainne bhuam-sa," ars' a' mhart, "gus a faigh thu ceanag bhon ghille shabhail ud thall a...

Chaidh e far a robh 'n gille sabhail.

"C'àite bheil thu dol?" ars' an gille sabhail.

"Ceanag bhon ghille shabhail, dh'ionnsaigh a' mhart, deuran bhon mhart dh'ionnsaigh a' chait, cat a ruitheas luch, luch a sgrìobas ìm, ìm chasa gadhar, gadhar a ruithe fiadh, fiadh a shnàmhas uisge, uisge fhliuchas clach, clach a mheileas tuagh, tuagh a ghearras slat, slat a ghabhas air Mearchan 's e 'n déidh mo chnothan ithe.

"O chan fhaigh thu ceanag fheòir bhuam-sa," ars' an gille sabhail "gus a faigh thu bonnach bhon bhean-taighe ud thall a dh'itheas mi."

Chaidh e far an robh a'bhean-taighe.

"Càite bheil thu dol?" ars a' bhean-taighe.

"Bonnach bhon bhean-taighe dh'ionnsaigh a' ghille sabhail, ceanag bhon ghille sabhail dh'ionnsaigh a' mhart, deuran bhon mhart dh'ionnsaigh a' chait, cat a ruitheas luch, luch a sgrìobas ìm, ìm chasa gadhar, gadhar a ruithe fiadh, fiadh a shnàmhas uisge, uisge fhliuchas clach, clach a mheileas tuagh, tuagh a ghearras slat, slat a ghabhas air Mearchan 's e 'n déidh mo chnothan ithe."

"O chan fhaigh thu bonnach bhuam-sa," arsa bean-an-taighe "gus an toir thu leat an criathar ud shìos 's gun téid thu sìos dhan an allt, agus gheibh thu làn do dh'uisge e."

Chaidh e sìos leis dhan allt.

"C'àite bheil thu dol?" ars an allta....

Co-dhiù thug e leis an criathar 's chaidh e sìos leis an allta. Lìon e suas an criathar le uisge, 's cha chumadh an criathar boinne.

Thàinig fìor-eun mór shuas os a chionn.

"Suath *moss* bog ris. Suath mas bog ris." Shuath esan *moss* bog ris 's cha chumadh an criathar boinne.

Thàinig fitheach mór os a chionn.

"Suath creadh ruadh rapach ris, suath creadh ruadh rapach ris." Shuath esan ris creadh a' chriathar 's thog e suas làn a' chriathar, 's lìon e 'n criathar le uisge. Fhuair e 'n t-uisge, 's thug e dhan bhean-taighe e, 's fhuair e 'm bonnach bho'n bhean-taighe 's thug e' m bonnach dhan ghille sabhail 's fhuair e ceanag fheòir bho'n ghille-sabhail 's thug e dhan mhart e, 's fhuair e 'n deuran bho'n mhart 's thug e dhan chat e... 's ruith an cat a' luch, luch a sgrìobas ìm, ìm chasa gadhar, gadhar a ruithe fiadh, fiadh a shnàmhas uisge, uisge fhliuchas clach, clach a mheileas tuagh. Dh'éirich e air Mearchan gus na thionndaidh an tòn aige dearg.

Frank, who told the tale at a considerable speed and with a fluency that could only have come from many hearings of it, had the immediate and undivided attention of the rest of the family. No one said a word about the fact that the one who had told it to them so often had himself just gone upstairs to bed, but from their reactions it was obvious that hearing this story brought back many pleasant and amusing childhood memories. Those in the company who did not have Gaelic were given no explanations, nor did they seem to need it, as they understood full well the significance it had once had in this home, the stronghold of Gaelic traditions. Though perfectly capable of offering a translation, such as follows here, Frank resumed the music, thus steering the course of the evening as his father had just done.

The direct translation of idiom from one language to another almost always produces a stilted effect with loss of the original impact. The following is therefore a close adaptation from the literal translation of the Gaelic version of the story. The sequence of motifs follows Frank MacArthur's Gaelic text, apart from where he unwittingly (and because of the speed at which he told it) omitted some of the items in the cumulative sequence. The sections added here to complete the text are indicated with square brackets, while words in round brackets are mine, added here to clarify meaning or to help the flow of the narrative:

Murchan and Mearchan (pronounced Moor-a-chan and Mar-a-chan, with the "ch" as in Loch.)

(Once upon a time) Murchan and Mearchan, so I heard, went to the woods for (hazel-)nuts, and as Murchan was up in the tree shaking them down, (so) Mearchan was eating them.
Down came Murchan from the tree and he asked Mearchan, "What did you do with all my nuts?"

"I ate them," said Mearchan.

"What's to be done with you (then)?"

"(There will be) a cane from down yonder, a cane from the wood up yonder whacking my backside."

"Where will I get a cane?"

He went to (a place) where there was a cane.

["Where are you going?" said the cane.

"For a cane to whack Mearchan for eating all my nuts."

"Oh, you won't get me," said the cane "until you get an axe to cut me."

So he went to where there was an axe.]

"Where are you going?" said the axe.

"For an axe to cut the cane to whack Mearchan for eating all my nuts."

"Oh, you won't get me," said the axe, "till you get a stone to grind me on."

He went to where there was a stone.

"Where are you going?" said the stone.

"For a stone to grind an axe, an axe to cut a cane, a cane for to whack Mearchan for eating all my nuts."

"Oh, you won't get me," said the stone, "until you fetch water to wet me."

He went (then) to where there was water.

"Where are you going?" said the water.

"For water to wet a stone, a stone to grind an axe, an axe for to cut a cane, a cane to whack Mearchan, who has eaten all my nuts."

"Oh, you won't get me," said the water, "until you get a deer that will swim me."

(So) he went to where there was a deer.

"Where are you going?" said the deer.

"For a deer to swim water, water to wet a stone, a stone to grind an axe, an axe to cut a cane, a cane to whack Mearchan, who has eaten all my nuts."

["Oh, you won't get me," said the deer, "until you get a hound that will chase me."

So he went to where there was a hound.

"Where are you going?" said the hound.

"For a hound that will chase a deer, a deer that will swim water, water to wet a stone, a stone to grind an axe, an axe to cut a cane, a cane to whack Mearchan, who has eaten all my nuts."

"Oh, you won't get me," said the hound, "until you get butter to smooth my feet."]

So he went to (a place) where there was butter.

"Where are you going?" said the butter.

"For butter for a hound's feet to chase a deer, a deer to swim water, water to wet a stone, a stone to grind an axe, an axe to cut a cane, a cane to whack Mearchan for eating all my nuts."

"Oh, you won't get me," said the butter, "until you get a mouse to scrape me."

So he went to where there was a mouse.

"Where are you going?" said the mouse.

"For a mouse to scrape butter, butter for a hound's feet, a hound to chase a deer, a deer to swim water, water to wet a stone, a stone to grind an axe, an axe to cut a cane, a cane to whack Mearchan for eating all my nuts."

"Oh, you won't get me," said the mouse, "until you get a cat to chase me."

So he went to where the cat was.

"Where are you going?" said the cat.

"For a cat to chase a mouse, a mouse to scrape butter, butter for a hound's feet, a hound to chase a deer, a deer to swim water, water to wet a stone, a stone to grind an axe, an axe to cut a cane, a cane to whack Mearchan, who has eaten all my nuts."

"Oh, you won't get me," said the cat, "until you get a drop of milk from the cow over there."

He went to where the cow was.

"Where are you going?" said the cow.

"For a drop of milk from you for the cat, for a cat to chase a mouse, a mouse to scrape butter, butter for a hound's feet, a hound to chase a deer, a deer to swim water, water to wet a stone, a stone to grind an axe, an axe to cut a cane, a cane to whack Mearchan, who as eaten all my nuts."

"Oh, you won't get a drop of milk from me," said the cow, "until you get a wisp of hay from the stable-boy over there at (Meadowside)."

So he went to where the stable-boy was.

"Where are you going?" said the stable-boy.

"For a wisp of hay for the cow that will give a drop of milk for the cat, a cat (that will) chase a mouse, a mouse to scrape butter, butter for a hound's feet, a hound to chase a deer, a deer to swim water, water to wet a stone, a stone to grind an axe, an axe to cut a cane, a cane to whack Mearchan, who has eaten all my nuts."

"Oh, you won't get a wisp of hay from me," said the stable-boy, "until you get a bannock for me to eat from the housewife over there."

He went to where the housewife was.

"Where are you going?" said the housewife.

"For a bannock from the housewife to feed the stable-boy, a wisp of hay from the stable-boy to feed the cow, a drop of milk from the cow for the cat, a cat to chase a mouse, a mouse to scrape butter, butter for a hound's feet, a hound to chase a deer, a deer to swim water, water to wet a stone, a stone to grind an axe, an axe to cut a cane, a cane to whack Mearchan for eating all my nuts."

"Oh, you won't get a bannock from me," said the housewife, "until you take that sieve over there and go down to the brook and fill it full of water."

He went down to the brook with it.

"Where are you going?" said the brook.

Anyway, he took the sieve with him, and went down into the brook with it. He filled the sieve up with water but it wouldn't hold any (liquid). Then a big eagle flew above his head.

"Rub (soft) wet stuff [moss] on it. Rub soft wet stuff on it."

So he rubbed it with soft wet stuff but the sieve wouldn't hold any (liquid).

Then came a big raven up above his head.

"Rub stiff red clay on it, rub stiff red clay on it."

So he rubbed stiff red clay on it and he lifted up the sieve full, and he filled the sieve with water. He got the water and he took it to the housewife, he got the bannock and he took it to the stable-boy, and he got the wisp of hay from the stable-boy and he took it to the cow; he got a drop of milk from the cow and he took it to the cat. And the cat chased the mouse, the mouse scraped the butter, the butter for the hound's feet, the hound chased the deer, the deer swam the water, the water wet the stone, the stone ground the axe, the axe cut the cane. And he set about Mearchan until his backside turned red!

The tale itself is an internationally recognized type of cumulative narrative, and one which was popular throughout Gaelic Scotland in various versions. Two such examples are contained in Robert C. MacLagan's *The Games and Diversions of Argyleshire*, published by the Folk-Lore Society in 1901.

"Murchan is Mearchan," like all cumulative tales, is an amusing story in which the children had to try and remember all the items in the sequence in which they were arranged in the tale. With Allan MacArthur's great emphasis upon accuracy of the memory, I could not but wonder if this tale, which his children so obviously enjoyed, was only one of his methods of exercising their memories while entertaining them at the same time. If this were, in fact, his aim then he certainly succeeded, as Frank had not recited it to his own children at bedtime (since his wife had no Gaelic, they adopted English as the language of their home), nor had he heard it since his own youth, when occasionally his father used to ask him to tell it to his younger brothers and sisters as he helped put them to bed.

Modern Legend

Storytelling had an important place in the MacArthur home, and Frank MacArthur described his father as having a 'wonderful memory' and noted that he could 'talk history' from morning till night. As long as Gaelic was spoken in their home, the MacArthurs were immersed in the oral traditions of the language. Throughout all except the last ten years of his life Allan MacArthur enjoyed hearing and telling *sgeulachdan*, the Gaelic word used to embrace all types of narrative, history, legend, and folktale alike, a word frequently used even when speaking English. As he told his stories he also took great pleasure in his ability to have complete hold over his audience, although he was reluctant to begin any story to which he felt he could not do justice because he had forgotten important details over the years.

In his old age, Allan modified his story repertoire to fit the everchanging interests of the community. His reputation as a good storyteller endured throughout his lifetime, regardless of the company he kept—Scots, French, or English alike—and he was invited to tell and retell accounts of events which had been relevant in the lives of all the inhabitants of the Valley.

In company, people tended to rely upon him for the accurate preservation of local history, such as this story, related here as a composite account, drawn from the dialogue in which it was told:

Many years ago, "I think it was in 1780," a Roman Catholic priest by the name of Father John Grant emigrated from Scotland to Cape Breton, Nova Scotia. With him he took a secret cure for healing skin cancer and he became well known as a "cancer doctor":

The Cape Breton Cancer Doctors

It's over one hundred years since my father had the cancer drawed. He had it in his mouth, and it wasn't this clergyman that did that; he was dead. And, eh...he had a servant girl, and whatever he used to do, you know, to draw the cancer, whatever it was, he gave the secret to this woman...girl that he had. And she kept on doing it. And then she married a fellow by the name of MacPherson; she was sixty years old then and he was only twenty-five years old! [Laughs] And when she died at eighty-four he took it up, you see, this MacPherson, and he lived to be eighty-four, curing the cancer, the same thing. Well now... Dan MacPherson that married...he married a girl from...I forget where—she was Irish. And he was curing...doing the same thing till he died. It was him that cured my cancer in 1917.

It was here [on the side of the face] and I had that one eight years before the roots started, but I knowed it was cancer before [that] because it would be like a little lump and it would be like somebody was hauling straw over your face, and you'd do like this [to rub it] and before your hand was down the pain would stop.... This eye got bloodshot before I went to Cape Breton to get it drawed....

Confidence in the cancer doctors was widespread, and the consensus of opinion was that interference from formally-trained medical doctors was to be avoided:

They couldn't do it, you see. He [MacPherson] would draw the cancer but they'd cut it out, you see. Aye, it was only a poor chance you'd get it then. It was all right to cut it out before the roots would start, but when the roots would start it's too late then. They could cut it out and you'd get better probably for a month or a couple of months, but it would be bound to start again and the next time it would be a lot worse, because you'd have more than one cancer, you see, with the roots spreading out. Well now, if they'd get something that would follow the roots and draw them back...but he [MacPherson]...whatever he was doing it would draw them back.

Using secret ingredients, MacPherson prepared a poultice-like application, 'a plaster', which he put on the cancer in order to 'draw it'. He would not allow his patients to have any knowledge of how he made it, but Allan was under the impression that he obtained the ingredients from a drug store. The plaster was applied to the skin and remained there from seven to nine days. At first, when it began to work it felt extremely painful, but it was said to draw the roots out and back into the main body of the cancer. Allan described this stage as being "like a black spider with legs." When the roots were finally drawn back into the body, the patient would be told that the cancer "dropped." This was not, however, the end of the treatment:

When the cancer would be killed...you'd have to wash it every day with some fresh milk, you see, and then you'd get half a teaspoonful of the essence of turpentine and you'd get the yolk of an egg and you'd put it in a small little dish and you'd mix it right till it formed a kind of a plaster. And when you'd wash it, then you'd take a little splinter or something, and you'd put this stuff all round the cancer, you see, and it would be cutting this lump—the cancer—from the proud flesh, and healing at the same time. And you'd have to follow that, and when it would get so small that it would be only flesh, you had to be careful then that you wouldn't break that, you see, because that was alive yet with cancer. You'd have to leave that till it would break by itself. When the cancer was killed, it would take the good out of you...you'd be worthless for three or four months, and you wasn't allowed to take any alcohol or anything like that, and you wasn't allowed to have wet feet or hands, or sweat, you know, like in the wintertime. I was three months, you know, and I had to take my time walking to the top of that hill. Well, there was something in that plaster that was going right through you, taking the good out of you.

The cancer patients were careful to follow up their treatment with the recommended preparations. None of them knew where the MacPherson got this idea but it is interesting to note that William Epps Cormack, who made the first journey across Newfoundland in 1821, wrote in his book that the Micmac Indians made a salve for skin ulcers that was composed of a mixture of turpentine and egg yolks.

In the early days of cancer curing, payment to the cancer doctor was little or nothing:

The people was poor then, they couldn't afford to pay. But it didn't matter whether you had money or not, they'd put a plaster to you. If you didn't have the money, well that was all right, they would treat your cancer just the same. Some would give him butter or something like that in payment, and they used to cure a lot that didn't pay at all.

This altered as the years went by and the cancer doctors began to have set charges for treatment. Latterly the cost to have a plaster applied to a cancer was $50. The last cancer doctor to practise cured only in her own home, which had been set up like a large clinic where the patients would stay until their treatment was completed. Besides the $50 for the plaster, she charged $5 a day for accommodation and care. Patients could expect to pay over $100 for their entire treatment, although it was generally agreed that the aim of the cancer doctor was to cure, not to make money.

Perhaps they'd be twenty people go to him in one night, and perhaps there might be two have cancer and the rest would go home free. If he wanted to make money he wouldn't turn away so many people—he'd draw whatever they had!

The success rate achieved by the cancer doctors was said to have been very high. Allan pointed out that the MacPhersons only took patients whom they were sure of treating successfully. If they considered that a cancer was 'too far gone' or if it had been treated first by a medical doctor, they wouldn't touch it:

He had to be very careful. If a person died and they [the relatives] kicked up a fuss, perhaps they'd blame him for killing him, and he'd be hung.

As may be expected, the activities of the cancer doctors eventually drew attention from the medical profession. At the nearest hospital—twenty-five miles away—one particular doctor made strong objections to MacPherson because he was "practising medicine without a licence," and sent the RCMP into the Codroy Valley to try to compel MacPherson to leave. Finally the medical doctor exerted such pressure that the cancer doctors were forced to abandon all visits to Newfoundland:

The doctor in Port aux Basques, Dr. B—, he was from England. He was in the First World War, you see; he was a war doctor. And he drove him [MacPherson] out. He wouldn't come back any more. MacPherson had a fellow from St. John's, he used to buy cattle around here, and he had cancer. His father was around South Branch and this doctor was there, you know. Not a [medical] doctor, but Dan MacPherson, the one that used to draw the cancer. And his son had cancer, because the doctors told him, and he got in contact with this MacPherson. He was at South Branch where he had about a dozen cases at that time, and he came. And, by God, Dr. B—, he happened to be up and he found out what this Dan MacPherson was doing. He went down, and this fellow had the plaster to him—Metcalf was his name; he was a butcher—and he only had the plaster on for four or five days when Dr. B— went out, and he had to close down. MacPherson had to show them everything because he was practising medicine without a licence. Well, he showed the doctor what he was at, and the doctor couldn't make anything of it; and MacPherson had to take the plaster off of him, and he went home. And he told the doctor, he said, 'You're killing this man,' he said, 'he'll be in his grave before three months time, and you are to be blamed; he can blame you for it.' Oh, he didn't believe that. He only lived two months when they got the word in South Branch that he died; his father sent word. Well, Dr. B—wasn't so stiff against MacPherson after that, but he stopped coming to Newfoundland on account of Dr. B—.

In the mid-1920s Allan worked at a sporting camp during the salmon fishing season (*see photo, page 89*). The Grand Codroy River had an unsurpassable reputation and attracted tourists and notable sportsmen from far and wide. For example, Allan's old friend, George Cormier, guided the late King George V. His own memorable encounter was not so much with a wealthy or noble sportsman but with a Scottish piper by the name of John MacPherson, who had accompanied a rich shipping agent to the camp. MacPherson was visiting Canada partly as guest of the shipping agent and partly in his professional capacity as piper. His role was to pipe ashore Scottish emigrants who were settling in Nova Scotia and to play at certain other functions. During their visit to Canada, the party went to Newfoundland to enjoy the salmon fishing of the Grand Codroy River. The arrival of the boat attracted attention from the newspapers, and more than fifty years later Allan MacArthur still had on his sitting room wall a reminder of the occasion: yellowed with age, it was a small newspaper clipping, unlabelled, undated (*right*), which any

—CHAMPION PIPER. — John Macpherson, of Newtonmore, Inverness, champion piper, son and grandson of champion pipers, who played the Athenia off when she sailed from the Old Country on a recent voyage with a large passenger list of settlers for Canada.

visitor could read: "CHAMPION PIPER—John MacPherson of Newtonmore, Inverness, champion piper, son and grandson of champion pipers, who played the Athenia off when she sailed from the Old Country on a recent voyage with a large passenger list of settlers for Canada." Allan spoke of their time in Newfoundland and suggested to me that perhaps I'd even know "this John MacPherson. Perhaps his people are still there?"

Two of Allan's sons, Jim and Frank, who were young lads at the time, also had vivid memories, and Frank told the story that his father had so often brought to mind:

The MacPherson Piper

Now about this John MacPherson, that piper that came to South Branch. Now Jimmy, he was only nine years old at the time. He was reasonably good on the pipes when he was nine. In fact, he used to have to put the big drone on the opposite side, you know, put it over his head, because he was small, and using the big pipes! And they used to kind of fall down over his shoulder, so he put the big drone on the opposite side of his head and hold them on that way. Jimmy learnt a tune from that man, and it goes like this—now I'm not sure that this is *exactly* the way *he* played it, and it may not be exactly the way Jimmy used to play it, but it's pretty close. And it goes like this: [5]

He was a tourist and he'd be fishing. He came out on a shipping line, I used to hear my father speak about it. This John MacPherson, he was supposed to be really a wonderful piper. But now it seems to be according to his picture that he must have been getting a bit old at the time.

He was impressed with Jimmy's piping, so much so that he wanted my father to let Jimmy go back to Scotland with him. But my grandmother, she wouldn't hear talk of it

Although Father was complimented by this—and he had reason to be complimented—I'm very doubtful if he'd be satisfied to let him go.[6]

Just as the experience stayed with Allan and his sons, so the question of "Who was this John MacPherson?" remained with me. Some fifteen years after photographing Allan's clipping, I took the opportunity of seeking information about him in the village of Newtonmore, the heart of MacPherson country. Following several unsuccessful attempts, I showed the photograph to Phosa MacPherson, a lady in her eighties. After a brief moment of hesitation, almost disbelief, she announced, "It's my father!" Phosa herself turned out to be none other than the granddaughter of the great Malcolm MacPherson, or *Calum Piobaire* as this most famous piobaireachd player was know. He was piper to Cluny MacPherson, Chief of the Clan MacPherson, and his son John (Phosa's father), took over this honourable position after his death. As the daughter of the hereditary piper to the Clan MacPherson, Phosa had a deep interest in piping. She wanted to know, of course, "who *was* this MacArthur in Newfoundland?" Her memories of her father's trip came flooding back at the sight of the photo and are recorded here as a fitting end to Allan's story:

It's quite a thrill to see that, because we didn't even know it had been taken! I'm *terribly* pleased to see it. And there was a very famous piping family by the name of MacArthur on Skye, you know.[7]

My father [John MacPherson] went with the Donaldsons to Nova Scotia. They went on the *Athenia*—it was a new ship of the Donaldson Line—that was its first trip out. And it was the first ship through the Strait of Belle Isle [that year] and my father said the icebergs were just enormous. But they had a wonderful holiday. They had three months fishing on and around the St. Lawrence, and camping. He had a wonderful holiday, and of course the pipes went with him—they went everywhere!

He was brought up in Laggan...his father was this famous piper taught by the MacCrimmons in Skye, because they originated there. And my great-grandfather came to Cluny as piper. He was Angus MacPherson, and Calum MacPherson was my father's father, and he was the piper to Cluny too. He taught my father two hundred pibrochs, and it wasn't off books or anything. It was all in his head.... My grandfather would play for hours and never repeat himself.

I've got a copy of an article from the *People's Friend*, September 26 1898 about him. [It's called] "Calum Pìòbaire— The World's Greatest Piobaireachd Player."

Music and the love of the pipes has lived on to the present generation of MacPhersons and MacArthurs—it's in the blood, they say. One surprising contrast, however, is that Phosa's father, the John MacPherson of the photo, was the last in her Scottish family to speak Gaelic, whereas it survived for two more generations in Allan MacArthur's Newfoundland family.

Storytelling as the old people knew it has changed considerably from what it was in Allan's day. The Gaelic language, along with the traditional tales and legends of the early settlers, have faded with his own generation. That is not to say, however, that storytelling has ceased to exist—it is, in fact, very much alive, generally in the form of local ancedote, and always told in English. Aspects of the old days are certainly incorporated by today's many entertaining narrators from all language backgrounds. It is not, however, the same essential part of a long winter evening's entertainment as it once was. The contrast is sharp: while nowadays the general entertainment in most homes comes by way of national television networks which telecast today's drama in technicolor, in the old days it was rather the delights of the imagination that could transport the listeners back into history, or to the realm of the supernatural or into an incredible adventure—all of this and more, aided only by the warmth of a hearth and good company.

CHAPTER 7

We Worked and We Sang

> Always singing! My mother would sing a song
> for every cow she'd milk.
> *Allan MacArthur, 1970*

W hile the Scots who emigrated to the New World in the nineteenth century may have suffered from material impoverishment, they were more than wealthy in their traditions of music and song. No hardships could restrict or bind this richness, a heritage of generations; and in this respect, the Codroy Valley Scots still closely resemble those who stayed behind in the Highlands. Exchanging a song or a tune is, for both peoples, as natural and spontaneous as sharing a piece of news, a favourite recipe, or an anecdote. It is part of everyday communication and has for countless centuries made a major and important contribution to the activities of the ceilidh.

As far as music and song are concerned, the main difference between Scotland and the Codroy Valley is that the enormous wealth of material found in the Valley is shared by all the ethnic groups—the Scots Gaels, French, Irish, and English alike. Throughout the history of the Valley, all made a significant contribution to the music and song at any ceilidh—and continue to do so today. This intermingling and sharing has been the pattern for about fifty years, from the time they began to blend their language groups at the milling (or waulking). By the turn of the century English was spoken by most people, albeit as a second language by many. There was, therefore, no barrier, and even today, people can still be heard referring phonetically to a particular song in Gaelic or French.

Allan MacArthur was generous and sincere in his praise of individual singers from all backgrounds. He had a genuine love of traditional music and song, and a deep interest in the "story behind the songs" he heard and sang. From his earliest childhood, the songs of his own people had the greatest influence. Typical of the Gaelic Highlander, Allan's songs had a function in every stage of life, from the cradle to the grave, and the countless days of toil in between were made lighter by the songs they had sung for generations.

The songs the old people brought from Scotland to the New World were of particular interest to Allan. Undoubtedly his family traditions went back through many generations:

Them songs came from Scotland. They were composed in Scotland, because my grandmother, you know, she was full of songs and my mother learned her songs. And my mother knowed sixty songs, and some they'd be double verses. She couldn't sing English songs, only all Gaelic songs. War songs and everything else. Oh, they're hard to sing, some of them, the war songs.... Well by gosh, I don't think I could sing any of them now. The most of these songs was in the time of Napoleon Bonepart, when he was fighting the British, you see, and Germany as well—Napoleon the First. When was the Battle of Waterloo fought...? It was 1815, wasn't it? Well, there was a song composed about Napoleon when he was on the Island of St. Helena, and what he did; "...on the eighteenth day of June my troops all in disorder, I could no longer stand defeat...." But it said he had 30,000 French, you see, when he runned away and went aboard the British ship; her name was the *Bellerophon*, and they took him to England.... Some of them wanted to kill him, you see, but some more of them didn't want that... and then from England they put him on the Island of St. Helena. And he was six years there before he died.

Now every song my mother knew, she knew why it was composed, and everything. There was a history behind the songs. Well, that was better than the song in a way because she would tell you first why the song was composed, and then she would sing the song, you know, to compare with the history, you see.

For Allan MacArthur and his generation their songs were their history books, preserving information of local and world politics without a page of print before them.

Allan was also interested in the composers of the songs. He had not only learned about the bards of Scotland from his elders, but also supplemented his knowledge with articles that appeared occasionally in Nova Scotia newspapers and, of course, in the biographies of his well-read copy of *Sàr-Obair*. Frank recalled that his father had a friend, Angus MacLellan from Cape Breton, who could read Gaelic. Whenever he visited them, Allan would ask him to read the *bardachd*, the poetry, aloud so that he might hear the examples of the composition of the great bards whose lives he had read about. He considered that the work of Scottish poets was of the very highest quality:

> "Well, I don't think there's any country in the world that can put down Scotland for their poetry. I don't think so."

Allan's son, Frank, who spent his first twelve years close to his grandmother, also has vivid memories of the place of song in the MacArthur home:

> And my grandmother, she could sit down, and Gaelic songs! She had songs twenty-four and twenty-five, and thirty verses— and it wasn't the four-lined verses; now that would be what we'd call an eight-line verse. Well now, she'd sit down in the nights with us, you know, and she'd be singing and telling us yarns, and stories.

There is no doubt that with the passing of Jenny MacArthur in 1931 many frequently sung songs were carried with her. Allan retained a large repertoire of his own, incorporating several of his mother's songs and many which he acquired independently. It was not that Allan did not know the same number of songs (for his entire song repertoire would have covered at least sixty, if not more), it was rather that he considered his mother's repertoire superior because many of her songs were long narrative and heroic songs which she retained all her life: "She had a lot of songs with no chorus in them, like war songs, you see, like that." But this type of song was probably the earliest victim of the changes in lifestyle brought about by modern trends, especially the coming of electricity and the increased tendency to socialize with mixed language groups.

In his youth Allan too could sing these fine old songs, but was disappointed that he could not "put one of them together now." He felt that during his old age he did not have the same interested audiences that his mother had had during her's, and this resulted in the loss of such songs, along with several stories. He was well aware of the fact that a memory which retains a large repertoire of songs and stories is only kept alive and accurate by the frequent singing of songs and the telling of stories. Indeed, without the audience a performer will be forced, as Allan MacArthur himself was, to allow certain sections of his repertoire to fade into the past. If only the tape recorder had arrived before the television set! "I wish I was ten years younger, I would keep you all day and all night singing songs!"

The songs which endured throughout Allan's life are those which were regularly used to accompany work in which every family participated, namely the wool-working:

> Some of the people that used to come from Scotland a hundred years ago, and more than that, you know, they used to bring sheep from Scotland. A little, but not too many, you see, because the journey was so far and so long, it would take so long.

For over a century the Valley has been known for its production of wool and woollen goods. Great changes have taken place through these years, and Allan witnessed most of them:

> They would shear the sheep in the spring—there was no men shearing then. I remember my father never sheared a sheep; my mother had to shear the sheep.

During his own lifetime, however, the men took what he considered to be a fairer share of the work, beginning with the shearing. At least until Confederation with Canada (1949) the women had to make almost all the clothes for the entire family, and as Allan put it, they "never wore anything only woollen clothes inside and outside." There was a tremendous amount of work to be done, and while singing lightened the work, it did not shorten the number of hours to be put in.

Until the turn of the century all the washed fleeces were hand-carded at home, generally through the long winter evenings at many a ceilidh and to many a story or song. In 1904, Gale's Carding Mill was built at Millville, and most families then opted to have their wool machine-carded, unless it was only a very small quantity.

George MacArthur washing fleeces to be sent to the mill, 1971.

Gale's Carding Mill, Millville, 1971.

The carding machines, 1971.

Songs were much more relevant to the next stage in the process—the spinning. Many of the first settlers were said to have brought their wheels with them from the Old Country, and the small 'Scotch wheel' was later adopted by the French who originally used the larger type (*right*). Just as in Scotland there were no songs kept solely for spinning; Allan said that his mother would choose her song "so it would suit the time." He distinguished between spinning songs and milling songs which, although they had a similar rhythmical flow, "were a little more military, you know, a little slower." Rhythm was important, for once a set, flowing rhythm was established, the work would keep on flowing and the yarn would rhythmically fill the bobbin on the wheel. Allan's recollection of his mother spinning was, like Frank's, closely linked to the song:

She was all the time singing, spinning... all the time singing. She had nothing but Gaelic, and most of them were Scotland's songs that she learnt from her mother.

In her old age, one of her favourite songs was "Dean Cadalan Samhach" (*page 179*), a lullaby with which she had also rocked her children and grandchildren to sleep:

The last time I heard it—well, my mother died in 1931—and the last time I heard it she was spinning at the wheel, and she was singing that song because it goes with the spinning, you see.

Spinning was generally done in the evening, and the whirr of the wheel could often be heard late into the night. Frank's vivid recollection of his grandmother clearly affirms the close bond between the work and the song:

And then, on the spinning wheel, you know, she used to be spinning, and when everyone else'd be gone to bed, you know, she'd spin and sing, sing, sing; she'd never spin unless she was singing.

Coping with the wool from fifty or more sheep was, to say the least, a daunting task! It was for this reason that the women of the Valley would hold several 'spinning bees' every summer in order to help neighbours with their workloads. Allan's wife, Mary, who had attended many of them, detailed the procedure.

They started early in the morning of an appointed day in summer when, "after the word had gone round," several men in the neighbourhood would harness up horse and cart and lift the family spinning wheel out to the cart. Accompanied then by wife or mother, they would set off to the house where the spinning bee was to be held. When several people had gathered, they would arrange all the wheels beside the house on a grassy area, set down chairs beside them, and the men would all leave for the rest of the day. All day

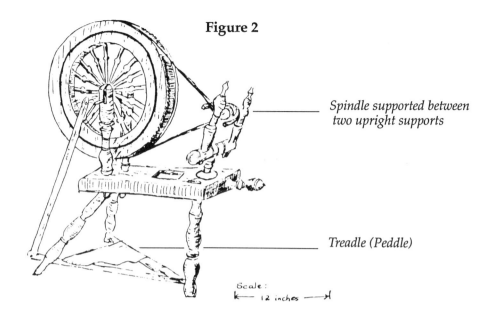

Figure 2

Spindle supported between
two upright supports

Treadle (Peddle)

Scale:
12 inches

Scotch spinning wheel of the type commonly used in the Codroy Valley.

Figure 3

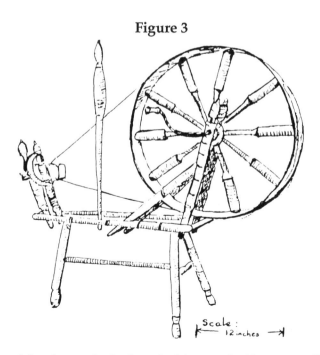

Scale:
12 inches

French hand-turned spinning wheel (operated without a treadle).

long, there would be a bustle of activity as a dozen or more women set to work on their neighbour's wool. An unthinkable task for one person to undertake, taking part in a spinning bee where there was a concentrated effort to complete this enormous amount of work in the one day was quite a different matter.

Mrs. MacArthur showed me a photograph of a spinning bee she attended in the 1930s, but it was not set up exactly as it would have been when they were working. The women all sat on chairs outside the house as they posed for the photograph. They were clad in the long shirts which were fashionable then, some wearing aprons, with a few spinning wheels arranged in the foreground. Mrs. MacArthur laughed as she recalled the enjoyment they used to get from going to a neighbour's spinning bee; not only was a tremendous amount of work accomplished, but they also experienced the great pleasure of getting together for a day's conversation, laughter, and singing—a rare luxury in a woman's life in those early days.

Not all the women at a spinning bee performed the same task, as the wool was never destined to be used all for the same purpose or for the one thickness or texture of cloth. The woman who held the spinning bee would decide how she wanted her wool: how much of it was to be spun finely, how much of it was to be wound into skeins for weaving, how much of the already-spun wool she wanted to be doubled and twisted into a thicker yarn to be knitted into heavy sweaters. The women then organized themselves according to the work that was required, no doubt taking advantage of the skill of the best spinners to do that one task throughout the day.

At midday the lady of the house provided food and drink for all her friends who helped. At the end of the day's work, around six o'clock, the men would all return to her house. The wool and the wheels would all be put away, and all the women, with their husbands, would sit in the kitchen where the housewife (as a token of her gratitude) would serve them all a hot, cooked meal of roasted meat and home-grown vegetables followed by an assortment of pies, bottled berries and tea. The company usually returned home after the meal, although occasionally they would stay on for a ceilidh.

The process of weaving was central to the domestic woollen industry, the finished article, and the songs—the main focus of this chapter.

Looms were also brought over from Scotland, though Cape Breton quickly became the main source for them. The Newfoundland Census Reports for the years 1901, 1911 and 1921 noted that there were as many as seventy weaving looms in the

Codroy Valley at one time, producing cloth valued at $3,476.[1] There is no indication of the yardage, but we might conclude that it was considerable. Though every home did not possess a loom, all had dealings with weavers. In the MacArthur home Allan's mother was relied upon for many years:

My mother used to weave as much as thirty yards of cloth, you see. You know, for pants—not for girls' petticoats or dresses or anything like that, that was different weaving, you see, well—with the yarn. When you'd be weaving for shirts, you see, it had to be thin, a little different. Well, that wouldn't be milled at all, but only the pants stuff. And even the women, they used to wear what they used to call the petticoats that was all made out of our wool too—*drogaid* we used to call it—what they used to weave for the men's shirts and the women. It was a different kind of weaving for that, you see, it was made lighter. We used to keep black sheep and white sheep. You'd make grey cloth out of the black wool and white wool, mix it together a lot and card it.... If you were making a chequered cloth out of it, well, it would probably be diamonds like, this way, well that was hard to make. We had weavers here that could weave six and seven yards in a day. Well, all that they were getting for that [was] ten cents a yard for every yard of cloth.

As far as Allan was concerned the expertise in weaving belonged to a French family, the Aucoins, originally from South Branch. He had the highest praise for one member of the family, Lucy (Mrs. George Cormier), whom he considered to be the pride of the Codroy Valley. Regarded by all with affection and esteem, in her day Lucy won many awards for her skilful weaving, including Lady Walwyn's silver trophy at the All-Newfoundland Exhibition held in St. John's in 1939.[2]

The *drògaid* (or drugget as it was called in English) was also a very popular cloth in Scotland. Although this lightweight material was ready to be cut and sewn as soon as it was woven, that was not the case for the heavier cloth. This heavy tweed, similar to *clò mór* in Scotland, was referred to as 'pants stuff' in the Codroy Valley. From it, they not only made pants [trousers] but also blankets and coats and any thick winter clothing. But this tweed had to undergo one final stage in the processing—the milling. No doubt the best remembered aspect of the Codroy Valley woollen industry, the millings brought all ethnic groups together, and without a doubt produced the largest body of songs, especially where Gaelic was concerned. This practice is basically the same as what is called 'waulking', 'fulling' or 'working' the cloth in different parts of the Highlands and Islands of Scotland, or *luadh* by Gaelic-speakers on both sides of the Atlantic. The tweed is milled in order to make it a thicker, tighter texture, so that clothes made from it would be warmer and more windproof. Although more than thirty years has passed since the last milling (or 'milling frolic', as it was sometimes called) was held in the Valley, many people still talk of these gatherings through the winter evenings when they worked together to the rhythm of countless songs. In spite of the fact that millings involved hard work, the people looked forward to them: "That was the fun! Many's the good time we had...."

Allan described the typical kitchen scene on such an evening. The owner of the cloth would have stitched the two ends of the roll together, making a huge loop of tweed, ready to be milled:

We had long planks about six or eight inches wide and benches under that, long enough.[3] Well, you double the cloth, perhaps you put two doubles of cloth. If you had thirty yards, you double to fifteen yards, that would be forty-five feet. Well, that would take quite a space, but not forty-five feet because you used to double the cloth up a little bit so you have enough in your hands, and the one [person] at the end was taking up probably about three yards of it because he had to keep it up on the end, at the same time from both sides. You'd strike on that side, and then when you'd put down the cloth we'd come down and strike on this side. It used to be thin first and then when you'd be milling like that it would thicken. You had to strike pretty hard on the table with it, and it had to be wet, you see, and soap on it. We used to put it in a tub and put it on those boards. Perhaps before you'd be through milling it you had to wet it a second time; it would mill better, because the dry cloth would never mill.

Then you could tell when you would measure it... the cloth that came out of the loom dry was thirty-six inches wide; well, you'd fix that up and mill it down to thirty-three or thirty-two inches. Whatever the women would say—they knowed when it was right. Well, they would measure the cloth and by the feeling of it, it was getting thick after milling so long, probably an hour and a half or two hours. And you had to work hard, and you had to be good to sing too. I seen some of the women do wonderful singing, and they wouldn't stop at one song at all; they would start another up, and then before the second one'd be over, you see the sweat'd be dropping off of everybody. And you daren't stop, you got to keep going! After every verse you're supposed to sing the chorus, you know, so all hands would sing the rounds. Oh you wouldn't hear yourself talking! You'd have to *stop* talkin', you see, when they would start, when they would be about fifteen or sixteen at one time, you know, with the loud voice! And they kept the beat with it.

The sweat would be falling off you before you'd be through! And then they would take it—the women knowed when it was milled enough for pants and coats and vests [waistcoats] and things like that. They had to measure the cloth, you know. When it would come out of the loom, well it would be so wide, you know, and so many inches wide [when it was milled]. Well, the women then they knowed more about it than the men, how to handle it.

The aim of the millings in the Codroy Valley with the rhythmic beating of the wet cloth on the boards was identical to the waulkings held in Scotland, but there were several basic differences. In the Highlands and Islands of Scotland, the waulking of the tweed was solely the work of the women, and indeed the attendance of men was taboo. As Charles W. Dunn points out in his *Highland Settler*, this was also the case in Cape Breton up until the turn of the century. Also, instead of dipping the tweed in a tub of soapy water, as described in the Codroy Valley, in Scotland it was, until this century, dipped in a tub of stale urine. According to John Lorne Campbell's account of waulking the tweed on the Isle of Barra, the Roman Catholics said a blessing, shaking water on the cloth in the name of the Trinity. However, none of these things are reported in the Codroy Valley. In fact, the entire notion of dipping the tweed in urine seemed incredible to those who were asked if they heard of it, and they would only show signs of believing it after being told that urine is excellent for removing the excess oil from the tweed and that it acts as a mordant to set the dye.

The most noticeable difference, however, is that all the songs at a Scottish waulking are in Gaelic, whereas the songs at Codroy Valley millings are in Gaelic, French, and English, and occasionally in a combination of two languages. These points were demonstrated to me at two 'staged' millings I attended—one in the kitchen of a MacArthur; the other in that of a Cormier—the intention was to replicate the work pattern and atmosphere of such an evening. There was no shortage of volunteers to take part, as all had once participated in the "real thing." Though all the participants were speaking English, their mannerisms and accents still indicated the cultures of origin.

Gaelic, French, and English singers were present, and having decided who would occupy the end seats (a 'Scotchman' at one and a Frenchman at the other on both occasions) everyone sat down on a bench by the table, took hold of the cloth, and the milling began. On one occasion the first song was a well-known Gaelic song, started by Frank MacArthur. He carried the verses while everyone else joined in the choruses. After a couple of wordless beats on the table, there followed a popular French song with a similar chorus, short verse, chorus pattern. After a rather tame beginning, which served to "get everyone in the mood," the milling was suddenly in full swing, with the singing as exuberant as one would expect and all hands beating vigorously.

Not all the songs were milling songs *per se*; many seem to have had their rhythms adapted to the beat required for the work. Nobody noticed my surprise, for example, when the Irish song "There Was an Old Woman from Wexford" and the English "Old King Cole" were presented as part of a predominantly Gaelic and French milling repertoire. It seemed as if these songs had long since been pressed into service to suit this occasion, and were ably fitted for the job.

Gaelic songs I knew from Scotland, such as "Ho-ró mo Nighean Donn Bhòidheach" ["Ho ro my Nut-brown Maiden" is an English adaptation] and "Fear a'Bhàta" ["The Boatman"] assumed a much quicker tempo in the Codroy Valley. It would be impossible to mill or waulk the tweed to either song in Scotland if, for example, one were to take a standard version of "Fear a' Bhàta" such as is printed in *A Choisir-Chiùil* where the singer is directed to sing "slowly, and with feeling."[4] Such adaptation of tempo goes back further than the folk memory—it may well be that they *were* sung at a quicker tempo in Scotland before a music publisher fixed the seemingly fitting directions to what are clearly love songs—it is simply impossible to identify the changes they have undergone since they migrated from the Old Country. These Gaelic songs are, however, fine examples of the very essence of oral tradition, representing the product of the 'folk process'—the wear and tear, adaptation and repair which over many years can be creatively applied to any tradition, oral or material. Not simply a collection of songs, the following pages are a colourful reflection of a way of life. Perhaps Allan MacArthur's own statement says it all: "And the story behind the song... well, that was better than the songs in a way...."

> *Illean Bithibh Sunndach* was composed in Scotland. It was a crowd that left the Eilean Sgiathanach, [Isle of Skye] leaving that and coming out in America, 'cross the Atlantic (I suppose it's the Atlantic they call it), crossing the Atlantic from those places, an t-Eilean Sgiathanach coming out, you know, in America.

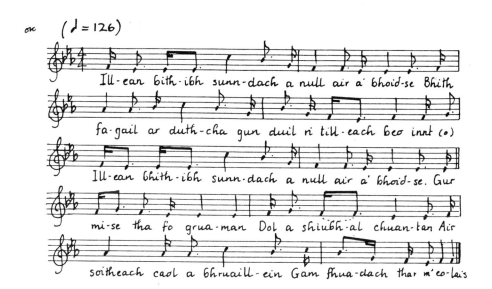

Illean Bithibh Sunndach

Chorus:

Illean bithibh sunndach a null air
   a' bhòidse
Bhith fàgail ar dùthcha gun dùil
   ri tilleadh beò innt
Illean bithibh sunndach a null air
   a' bhòidse.

1 Gur mise tha fo ghruaman
   Dol a shiubhal chuantan
   Air soitheach caol a' bhruaillein
   Gam fhuadach thar m'eòlais.

2 'S mise tha fo mhi-thoileachd
   O'n dh'fhàg mi'n t-Eilean
      Sgitheanach
   'S thoir dùrachd mo
      chridhe-sa
   Dhan nighean dh'fhàg mi
   brònach.

3 Illean cridheil gaolach
      Togaibh rith' a h-aodach
   Chan fhaigh mi 'n tìr mo ghaoil
      sibh
   Cho slaoidhte an am seòlaidh.

4 Illean cridheil togarrach

Boys Be Happy

Chorus:

Boys be happy going over on the
   voyage
Leaving our land without hope
   of returning alive to it
Boys be happy going over on the
   voyage.

1 It is me that's gloomy
   Going to sail the seas
   In the slender storm-tossed vessel
   Sending me away from my
      kindred.

2 I am without happiness
   Since I left the Isle of Skye
   Take my heartfelt blessings
   To the maid who left me sad.

3 Happy dear lads
   Put up her sails
   I do not find you in the land of
      my love
   So sluggish at the time of sailing.

4 Hearty happy lads

4 Illean cridheil togarrach
Olaidh sibh na thogaras
Oir 's ann an Tobar Mhoire
Ni sinn coinneamh ris a'
   chòmhlan.

5 Illean cridheil ceanalta
Deanaibh riof a theannachadh
Dar thig an stoirm an
   ath-bhliadhna
Bu mhath dhuinn a bhith
   còmhla.

6 Gur mise tha fo éislein
Ri còmhdhail na....
O'n d'fhàg mi thu, eudail
Air féill an Inbhir Lòchaidh.

7 'S ioma rud a chunna mi
Tha cuir móran mulaid orm
An diugh gun d'rinn iad tuilleadh
   dheth
MacDhùghaill bhith 'na chòcair.

8 Gur mis tha fo ghràin dheth
Dar chi mi fear dubh grànda
'S ann theannas mi ri ràinich
Nuair chi mi barr a mheòirean

9 Dar ruigeas sinn Ameireaga
Cha bhi dìth no deireas oirnn
Gu faigh sinn pailteas coilleadh
Ann an Eilean Nova Sgòisi.

Drink as much as you like
It will be in Tobermory
We shall meet the crowd (group).

5 Hearty affectionate lads
Tighten a reef
When the storm comes next year
It would be good for us to be
   together.

6 It is I who am downhearted
Meeting the....
Since I left you, my dear one
At the fair in Inverlochy.

7 Many a thing I have seen
That makes me sad
Today they have made it even
   worse
And put MacDougall in the
   galley (doing the cooking).

8 It is I who am repelled
When I see an ugly black
   (haired?) man
I start to cry
When I see his (dirty) fingernails.

9 When we get to America
We shall not want or be short of
   anything
We'll find plenty wood
In the Isle of Nova Scotia.

A Scottish variant of the same song was collected in Moidart (where Allan's ancestors came from) by the late Dr. Calum MacLean of the School of Scottish Studies. There are interesting differences in this text, and though the melody is very similar, the song is sung at a considerably slower tempo.

ok (♩ = 116)

Gu-ra boi-dheach am ba-ta Bhith 'ga feith-eamh aig sai-le
Nuair a theid na siuil bha-na A cha-radh ri cruinn.

Gura Boidheach am Bata

Chorus

Gura bòidheach am bàta
Bhith 'ga feitheamh aig sàile
Nuair a théid na siùil bhàna
A chàradh ri cruinn.

1 Dar a thog sinn an t-acair
'S a chaidh i fo astar
Cha b'e gillean gun tapachd
A smachdaicheadh i.

2 Nuair a thug sinn gu cuan i
'S i air bharr nan tonn uaine
'S i 'ga fàgail air fuaradh
Gus na dh 'fhuadaicheadh sinn.

3 Chaidh i roimh na caoiltean
'S i cho luath ris a' ghaothaidh
'S chum na gillean rith' h-aodach
Gus na (? sgaoil i fo? druim).

4 Labhair Eóghain mo bhràthair
"Deanaibh riofadh gu làidir
Saoil an dean i ar bàthadh
Fhad 's bhios sàile fo druim?"

5 A' dol timcheall air Seona
Dh'fhàs an fhairrge glé
    ghreannmhor
Dh'iarr na gillean *reef-hank*
A chur gu teann 's an t-seòl chinn.

6 Seachad beulaibh Dhun Oraigh
Chaidh a riofadh gu dòigheil
'S e bhith 'g éisdeachd a crònain
Ceòl bu deònaiche leinn.

7 Nuair a chuir sinn gu port i
S a dh'fheuch sinn a cosnadh
'S ó gu feumadh i doctair
Fhuair i lot...cinn.

8 Dar a bha mi 's a' ghàbhadh
Rinn mi smaointean neo dhà ann
Mo leannan 's mo chàirdean
Bhith 'ga fàgail dha'm chaoidh.

9 Nam biodh fhios aig mo
    mhàthair
Dar a bha mi 's a'ghàbhadh
Bhiodh i guidhe gu làidir
Righ nan Gràs a bhith leinn.

Bonnie Is the Ship

Chorus:

Bonnie is the ship, as we await her
    at sea
When the white sails are folded to
    her masts.

1 When we lifted the anchor
And gathered speed
They would have to be brave boys
Who could control her.

2 When we took her out to sea
[Sailing] on top of the green
    waves
Being held to the windward side
Until we were driven before the
    wind.

3 It went through the narrows
As swift as the wind
The boys kept adding sail
Until she (?—under her? keel).

4 My brother Ewan said
"Tie the rope securely
I wonder if it will drown us
As long as there is sea water
    under her keel?"

5 Going round Shona
The sea became very stormy
The boys asked for a reef hank
To be put securely in the topsail.

6 Passing by Dun Oraigh
They got her well and truly reefed
Listening to her humming along
Was the music we liked best.

7 When we turned her to port
And tried to get her under control
Oh she would need a doctor
She got a wound...her head.

8 When I was in danger
I had a thought or two
My sweetheart and my friends
Would be left mourning me.

9 If my mother had known
When we encountered danger
She would have earnestly prayed
That God of Grace be with us.

10 Dar a ràine sinn Grianaig
   Taighean cusbainn 'gan clìoradh
   Uisge-beatha cha b'fhiach e
   Ach am fion 'ga thoirt dhuinn.

11 Gheibh sinn canabhas ùr dhi
   Agus rudan bho'n bhùthaidh
   Cruinn ghasda 'n a' ghiùthsaich
   'S nach lùb gun droch shìd.

10 When we reached Greenock
   Clearing Customs houses
   Whisky wasn't good enough
   It was wine they gave us.

11 We shall get her new canvas
   And things from the shop
   Fine masts of fir
   Won't bend without bad
   weather.

A song "from the old people," these words also relate details of the emigration from Scotland. Allan got it from his mother and one might assume that it was composed during that stage in their history as it is not, to my knowledge, found in any Scottish collection.

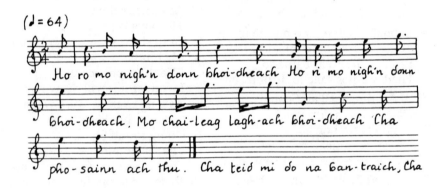

Ho Ro Mo Nighean Donn Bhoidheach
(Allan's Version)

Chorus:
Ho rò mo nighean donn
   bhòidheach
Ho rì mo nighean donn
   bhòidheach
Mo chaileag laghach bhòidheach
Cha phòs mi ach thù.

1 'S a Pheigi dhonn nam blàth-shuil
   Gur h-òg a thug mi gràdh dhut
   Gur h-iomadh gaol is àilleas
   Tha ghnàth tighinn bho d'ghnùis.

Ho Ro My Brown-Haired Maiden

Chorus:
Ho ro my brown-haired maiden
Ho ri my brown-haired maiden
My sweet and lovely maiden
I'll marry none but you.

1 Brown-haired Peggy with the
      warm eyes
   I was young when I fell in love
      with you
   Much love and beauty
   Shines always in your face.

2 Di-Dòmhnaich dol dhan
t-searmon
Chan fhaic fear eile cearb ort
Bidh ribein geal is dearg ort
'Na chàradh gu dlùth.

3 'Se 'n stòp a rinn mo bhristeadh
'Se'n t-òl a dh'fhàg gun mheas mi
Mo thruaigh an té gheibh mise
Bidh uisg air a sùil.

4 'S a riamh bho'n dh'fhàg mi
d'fhianais
Gu bheil mi dubhach cianail
Mo chridhe trom gam phianadh
Le iargain do rùin.

2 On Sunday going to the sermon
Nobody ever sees imperfections
in your dress
You will have white and red
ribbons
Tied firmly in place.

3 It's the bottle that has broken me
[was my downfall]
The drinking left me without
respect
Pity the one who gets me
She'll have tears in her eyes.

4 Ever since I lost sight of you
I am sad and lonely
My heart is heavy and painful
Longing for your love.

Ho Ro My Brown-Haired Maiden
(Frank's Version:)

Chorus:

Ho ró mo nighean donn
bhòidheach,
Ho rì mo nighean donn
bhòidheach,
Mo chaileag laghach, bhoidheach,
Cha phòsainn ach thu.

1 Cha téid mi do na bantraich,
Cha téid gu de bheir ann mi;
A Pheigi 's tu bheir ann mi,
'S ann ann tha mo rùn.

2 'S e 'n t-òl a dh'fhag gun mheas
mi,
'S e 'n t-òl a bhris mo chrìdh.
Mo thruaigh an té gheibh mise,
Bidh uisg' air a sùil.

3 I asked her if she loved me
She said she was above me;
She opened the door and shoved
me,
And called me a fool.

4 Ho ro my dark-eyed maiden,
Ho ri my dark-eyed maiden,
Ho ro my dark-eyed maiden,
I would only marry you.

Ho ro My Brown-Haired Maiden

Chorus:

Ho ro my brown-haired maiden,
Ho ri my brown-haired maiden,
My sweet and lovely maiden
I'll marry none but you.

1 I will not go to the widow's
I will not, whatever would take
me there
It's for you, Peggy, I would go
there
That's where my choice lies.

2 The drink has left me without
respect
The drink has broken my heart
Pity the one who gets me
She will have tears in her eye.

[The remaining verses are in
English.]

While the song is immediately recognizable as one of the most familiar Gaelic songs, long since standardized in print in numerous Scottish song collections, the versions here can be said to belong to the Codroy Valley Scots. Whether the Gaelic text left Scotland exactly as sung here and escaped the enforced Scottish standardization, or whether it acquired its own interesting uniqueness in the New World, who can tell? Nowadays, it is still very popular in the Valley, referred to by its Gaelic title, classified as a milling song, and often played on the accordion or fiddle. It is occasionally sung with the English words "Ho ro my dark-eyed maiden / My bonnie dark-eyed maiden / I would only marry you," a pleasant alternative to Professor J. Stuart Blackie's "Ho ro My Nut-Brown Maiden," which has caught on in Scotland.

Mhairi Dhubh na Hu o Ho
Chorus:
A Mhàiri Dhubh na hù o hó
A Mhàiri Dhubh o rio ró
A Mhàiri Dhubh na hù o hó
Tha m'inntinn trom bho'n
    dhealaich mi
Ri Mairi Dhubh o hù o hó.

1 Latha dhomh 's mi dol air sràid
  Co thachair orm ach mo ghràdh
  O gu dearbh cha tog thu làmh
  Cha bhi mi slàn mur faigh mi
    thu.

Black-Haired Mary
Chorus:
My black-haired Mary na hu o ho
My black-haired Mary na hu o ho
My black-haired Mary na hu o ho
My mind is heavy since we parted

1 One day when I was walking
  Who should I meet but my love
  O surely you have not given your
    hand
  I shall not thrive if I can't have
    you.

2 It is you that has such

2 'S ann ort fhéin a dh'fhàs a'
     ghruag
   Fidheachanan sìos mud' chluais
   Ribeinnean 'ga chumail suas
   Is prìne cinn 'ga theannachadh.

3 Fhad's a chì mo shuil a ghrian
   Tighinn bho'n ear 's a' dol an iar
   Air fear liath cha bhi mo mhiann
   'S na ciabhagan a' tanachadh.

4 Mhàiri lurach anns a' ghleann
   Aig a bheil a' mhala chaol
   'Sann a mach Airigh nan Caol
   A thug mi'n gaol nach b'aithreach
     leam.

5 'S truagh nach mis' is tu fhéin
   Bha 'sa' ghleann far 'm biodh na
     féidh
   'S binn thu na 'n fhidheall air
     ghleus
   'S am beus an déidh a
     theannachadh.

6 'S truagh nach mise bha fo'n
     fhòid
   Ann an ciste chaol nam bòrd
   Man tug mi mo ghaol cho mór
   A sheòladair na mharaiche.

(beautiful) hair
Plaits down round your ears
Ribbons tying it up.
And a hairpin tightening it.

3 As long as my eye can see the
     sun
   Coming from the east and
     setting in the west
   A grey-haired man will not
     attract me
   With his locks getting thinner.

4 Lovely Mary in the glen
   Who has the slender [eye]brow(s)
   It was out on Airigh nan Caol
   I gave the love I haven't regretted.

5 It's a pity that you and I were not
   In the glen where the deer are
   You are sweeter-voiced than a
     well-tuned fiddle
   With the base [string] tightened.

6 I wish I were under the sod
   In a narrow wooden coffin
   Before I gave the love so great
   To a sailor or a seaman.

The text of this song may well make the listener (or reader) wonder whether it was a man or woman who composed it. Waulking songs in Scotland were generally the composition of women, and over many generations of oral transmission the texts that survive are quite often disjointed and may incorporate complete passages from other songs. It would not be unusual, then, for song text to display apparent confusion as to who is singing it, male or female. This song is a particularly complex example. Considering the fact that in the New World men were included at the milling, it is not surprising that many of the songs recorded there are ones in which men take a leading role, yet still display the traditional poetry of women.

On the day Allan recorded this song he was in the company of three of his sons; George, Martin, and John. Although more than twenty years had passed since there had been a milling in their house (or in the Valley) they spontaneously took hold of the tablecloth along with their father, and to the vigorous beating of the cloth on the table, Allan sang the verses and the boys 'lifted' the chorus. Inseparable from each other, the song was part of the work; and the work not only belonged to the song, but had sustained it with constant singing throughout their lives.

The singing of "Mhairi Dhubh na Hu a Ho"—was an immediate re-creation of the atmosphere of the milling—total unity and enjoyment. It may well have been Allan's intention to take a well-deserved break, but no sooner had the last thump of the final chorus hit the table than the boys followed with the rhythm a few customary songless beats on the 'boards'. With flawless timing (and obvious enjoyment), George launched forth into the next song, knowing full well that his father would pick up the verse the moment the boys finished the chorus.

While I had never within my own generation in Scotland witnessed this virtually automatic hand action to accompany waulking/milling songs sung merely for pleasure (as opposed to work), yet it was certainly remembered by older people. A centuries-old custom, this is interestingly documented by John Ramsey of Ochtertyre in his book *Scotland and Scotsmen in the Eighteenth Century*:

> When the same airs are sung in their hours of relaxation, the time is marked by the motion of a napkin which all performers lay hold of. In singing, one person leads the band, but in a certain part of the tune he stops to take breath, while the rest strike in and complete the air by pronouncing to it a chorus of words and syllables....[5]

Ol an deoch air làmh mo rùin
Chorus:
Ol an deoch air làmh mo rùin
Deoch slàint' air fear an tùir
Ol an deoch air làmh mo rùin.

Drink to the Health of my Love
Chorus:
Drink to the health of my love
Health to the man of the tower
Drink to the health of my love.

1 'S mi a' leigeil as na seisreach
Tha'm feasgar a' leagadh
driùchd.

2 Oladh ga nach òladh càch i
Biodh mo phàirt-as 'n ceann a'
bhùird.

1 As I loose the plough team
The evening is shedding dew.

2 Whether or not others will drink
it
My portion will be at the head of
the table.

This song, though short, is an interesting version of the same song collected from Peter Stewart of Uig, Isle of Skye, by Marjory Kennedy-Fraser in 1909. Of particular interest and delight to me is that Peter Stewart is my great- grandfather; and though many Gaelic songs were passed on orally to my own generation this one, albeit committed to print, had vanished from my family. It had somehow escaped oral transmission and was then only accessible as 'an arrangement by Kennedy-Fraser. Versions of it, however, are found in several parts of Gaelic Scotland.

Hù a Hù Ailein Duinn
Chorus:
Hù a hù Ailein Duinn
Ailein Duinn bhòidhich
'S a hù a hù Ailein Duinn.

1 Ailein Duinn a' chùil dualaich
Bhuidhe chuachagaich bhòidhich

2 Ailein Duinn a' chùil bhuidhe
Bhith 'gad chùmha 's tu
brònach.

3 'S truagh nach robh mi 's an
fhiabhras
Man d'fhuair mi riamh beò thu.

Handsome Alan Donn
Chorus:
Hu a hu Alan Donn
Handsome Alan Donn
'S hu a hu Alan Donn.

1 Allan Donn with the lovely hair
Yellow and very curly.

2 Alan Donn of the yellow hair
Lamenting for you in your
sorrow.

3 It's a pity I wasn't sick with
fever
Before I ever found you alive.

Another song from his mother's repertoire, Allan also sang this one at a ceilidh with the company joining in the chorus. He had already made reference to the fact that there were a lot of songs from the Napoleonic Wars, and in fact this one is a melodic variant of a Skye song, usually called "Och ho ró o Ille Dhuinn," which appears to allude to the Egyptian campaign of 1798. The style of Allan's song, however, belongs to an earlier age, probably the seventeenth century. Although it is not, so far as I know, in any Scottish collection, it has been recorded by John Shaw from a Gaelic singer in Cape Breton who said there was an old MacArthur with a lot of songs whose peoople were from Canna.

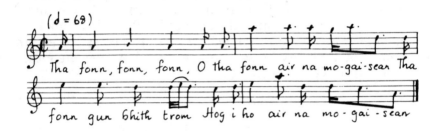

Oran nam Mogaisean

Chorus:
Tha fonn, fonn, fonn air
O tha fonn air na mogaisean
Tha fonn gun bhith trom
Hog i ó air na mogaisean.

1 Thòisich Seumas Ryan
   'S rinn e (?croicean) do
       mhogaisean
   Gun d'chart e dhiùbh na
       h-aobrainn
   'S cha robh iad craobhaidh
       fhathast air.

2 Theid mi sìos do'n aifhrionn
   An coibhneas nan caileagan
   Cha ghabh iad facal ùrnuigh
   Ach sùil air mo mhogaisean.

   ...

The Song of the Moccasins

Chorus:
Let's sing, sing, sing
Let's sing about the moccasins
A song that is not sad
[Let's sing] about the moccasins.

1 James Ryan began
   And he made (a kind of ?)
       moccasin
   He cut them off at the ankles
   And they still did not fit him too
       well.

2 I went down to Mass
   In the cheerful company of the
       girls
   They won't say a word of prayer
   For looking at my moccasins.

3 Neil MacGuarry said
   Did you ever get..
       .....
       .....

4 Fhuair mi craiceann caorach
  'S dùil rium caol a ghearradh as
  Thilg mi an dara taobh e
  Ach fhuair mi laoicionn
    gamhnach.

4 I got a sheep skin
  Thinking to cut a strip out of it
  I threw it to one side
  But I got a piece of cowhide.

Allan's brother, Murdoch, composed this song in the Codroy Valley. When he considered that he didn't have a great deal of success at making moccasins, he decided he might as well compose a song about them. Although Allan said he had forgotten most of the verses, yet what he could recall and the "story behind it" is worth preserving. A further version from Cape Breton (which acknowledges the Codroy Valley as its source) is in Volume 2 of Donald A. Ferguson's collection, *Fad air Falbh as Innse Gall: Beyond the Hebrides*, published in Halifax, Nova Scotia in 1977. It obviously 'caught on' there, and additional verses were added by a Cape Bretoner.

Allan's background information on the song tells also of a craft that has died out in the Codroy Valley:

He made a pair of moccasins and it took him quite a while to make them, you know. Of course, the moccasins they're out o' style since years around here, but he made the moccasins like that, you know, out of cowhide. You had to stretch the cowhide (after you'd kill the animal) on a wall or something, till it was dry, and then you would cut out the strip around eight inches wide and twenty-four inches long and then you'd scrape the hair off it with a sharp knife or even with glass. Then you'd take the rough off a' the outside and you'd plane it, you know, with the plane to make it smooth leather from the hide.

And we used to tan it in bark. Birch bark, oh yes. We used to take that off o' the trees, you know, and in June and July when the sap would be outside of the wood, you see, next to the bark, it was no trouble to peel the bark off in big slices, probably that long [indicating three feet], and probably twelve inches wide or something like that. Of course, you'd have to soak the hide first, you see. You'd split it in the centre and put it in a great big puncheon and put the bark on to it and water, and that's the way. Leave it for a few days, probably four days the first time, then you'd throw the water away and throw all the bark away, set it in again, you know, and the third time you'd leave it probably for a fortnight, and the leather would be tanned then, you see, fit to use. It would stain the leather brown.

Oh, well, I suppose it's thirty-five years since I didn't tan any leather. And sheepskin we used to tan and calfskin, you know,

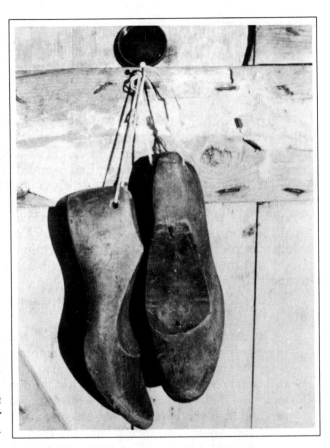

Allan's wooden lasts for shoes or moccasins.

that would be wonderful for leggings or for dress boots, or anything like that. You'd make shoes out of that, calf leather and everything else. Well, my father, he was a shoemaker in a way—he could make all kinds of shoes. Yes, even used to make the boots we used to wear up to the knees, but he had the last, purposed for that, you see.

And they were awful hard to make, you see, because it was so long, this way, going out that way, and then you had to cramp the leather, you know, so it would cramp around the heel. This would be all in one piece from that [pointing to the ankle] right up to here [the knee], and you had to cramp it around the toe, you see, on these lasts. But he could do it, you know.

And this was the song about the moccasins that Murdoch composed over forty years ago.

Ideally suited to the milling table, the song never failed to create much amusement as the story was well-known by the older folk who remembered Murdoch.

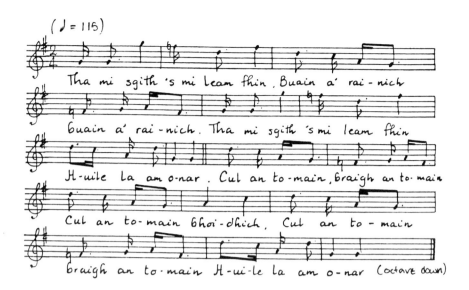

Buain a' Rainich	Cutting Bracken
Chorus:	*Chorus:*
Tha mi sgìth 's mi leam fhìn	I am tired and alone
Buain a' rainich buain a' rainich	Cutting bracken, cutting bracken
Tha mi sgìth 's mi leam fhìn	I am tired and alone
H-uile la am ònar.	Every day on my own.
1 Cùl an tomain, bràigh an tomain	1 At the back of the hillock, at the top of the hillock
Cùl an tomain bhòidhich	At the back of the beautiful hillock
Cùl am tomain, bràigh an tomain	At the top of the hillock, at the top of the hillock
H-uile là am ònar.	Every day on my own.

Well known in Scotland, but usually at a much slower pace, this song was written down by Frances Tolmie on Skye in 1843. There it might have been used for spinning, but not for waulking or milling as it was in the Codroy Valley.

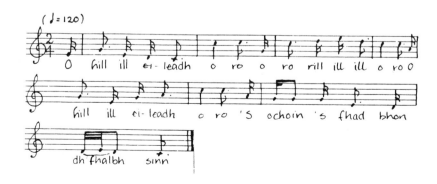

O hill ill eileadh o ro

Chorus:
O hill ill éileadh ó ro
O ró rill ill ill ó ro
O hill ill éileadh ó ro
'S ochóin 's fhad bhon dh'fhalbh
    sinn.

1 An oidhche sin a bha sinn
    Ri port an Ceann Loch Alainn
    Bha 'n t-sìde greannach...
    'S i làidir o'n earr-dheas.

2 'S an oidhche sin a bha sinn
    A staigh an ceann a' Chàrnain
    Bha'n t-sìde teannadh fàbhrach
    'S i blàth gun bhith dorcha.

3 Nuair thog sinn rithe h-aodach
    Bho bharr a cranna caola
    Cha robh ann do ghaoth ach
    Na bheireadh taobh air falbh sinn.

4 'S cha d'rinn sinn dad ach
      gluasad
    Na rinn m'an ghealaich buaile
    Bha riobainn ruadh is uaine
    'S iad gruamach gu soirbheas.

5 Dol seachad air Beinn
      Bhòidheach
    Thug sinn troigh a sgod dhi
    'S ann dhi bu bheag mo chòta
    Dar chuir i stròin do'n earr-dheas.

6 Dol seachad Rudha Réidh
      dhuinn
    Nuair bhuail a' ghaoth gu
      séideadh ——
    'S an fheasgar gu robh feum air
    Nuair dh'éirich an fhairrge.

7 B'e 'm maighistir 'ga stiùireadh
    Gilleasbuig gille Iain Dhùghaill?
    'S mi fhìn an cois an t-siùil
    Is mo shùil air an earr-dheas.

O hill ill eileadh o ro

Chorus
O hill ill eileadh o ro
O ro rill ill ill or ro
O hill ill eileadh o ro
Alas it is long since we left.

1 That night when we were
    In port at the head of Loch Alainn
    The weather was unpleasant
      [angry]
    With a strong southeasterly wind.

2 And the night that we were
    In at the head of Carnan
    The weather turned favourable
    Warm and not dark.

3 When he hoisted her sails
    From the top of her masts
    There was only sufficient wind
    To get us going.

4 And we had hardly moved
    When the moon put a halo
      round herself
    There was a straggle of red and
      green [ribbon]
    Giving a warning of wind.

5 As we passed Beinn Bhoidheach
    We gave her a foot of sheet
    My amount of coat was little
      enough for her
    As she headed south-eastwards.

6 As we passed Reidh Point
    The wind rose to gale force
    In the evening there was need of it
    When the seas rose.

7 The skipper who sailed her
    Was Gillespie, John son of
      Dougald's boy
    I was at the sail
    And my eye on the southeast.

Allan was quite adamant that he was not the only person who knew Gaelic songs, and when we visited his old friend, Sandy Francis (Sandy MacIsaac of St. Andrews), Allan prompted him to sing the above song. Allan referred to it as "Sandy's song," and the recording has several men of that generation enthusiastically singing with Sandy. The same melody with a variant text is known in Cape Breton (e.g. collector John Shaw has recorded it) and there are Scottish variants of the text.[6] There seems to be an obvious connection between this song and "Am Bata Raineach" by Duncan Johnston. This would suggest, then, that Sandy's song is probably much older than the modern twentieth-century comparison, as Duncan Johnston borrowed freely from existing tradition to compose many of his well-loved Gaelic songs which have been popularized on modern platforms.

Ged Tha Mi Gun Chrodh Gun Aighean

Chorus:
Ged tha mi gun chrodh, gun aighean.
Gun chrodh laoigh, gun chaoraich agam;
Ged the mi gun chrodh, gun aighean
Geibh mi fhathast òigear grìnn.

1 Ged tha mi gun chrodh, gun chaoraich,
   Chan'eil mi gun bhòidhchead aodainn.
   Dheannain breacan a bhiodh saor dhuit,
   Agus aodach a bhiodh grìnn.

(Repeat chorus—Ged tha mi....)

Though I am without Cattle or Heifers

Chorus:
Though I am without cattle or heifers
Without any cows in calf, or sheep
Though I am without cattle or heifers
I shall yet find a fine young man.

1 Though I am without cattle or sheep
   I am not without a bonny face
   I would make you a plaid that was inexpensive
   And some very fine clothes.

Of unknown authorship, "Gun Chrodh Gun Aighean" appears in many Gaelic song collections. This fragment which Frank remembered from his father's singing is a milling song; again, it is much quicker than the same song which is sung in Scotland.

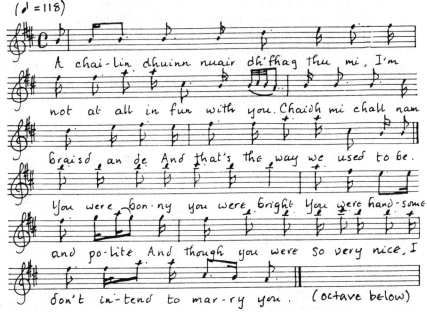

A chai-lin dhuinn nuair dh'fhag thu mi, I'm not at all in fun with you. Chaidh mi chall nam braisd an de And that's the way we used to be. You were bon-ny you were bright You were hand-some and po-lite And though you were so very nice, I don't in-tend to mar-ry you. *(octave below)*

A Chailin Dhuinn Nuair Dh'fhag Thu Mi

Chorus:
A chailin dhuinn bhon dh'fhàg
thu mi
I'm not at all in fun with you
Chaidh mi [chall nam braisd?] an dé
And that's the way we used to be.

1 You were bonnie, you were
bright
You were handsome and polite
And though you were so very nice
I don't intend to marry you.

2 If I had wings like a dove
I would fly the airs above
I would go to see my love
Who left me dull this evening.

3 Many a one that I had run
Since the first that I begun
I will try the best I can
To rig a plan of leaving you.

Brown-Haired Maiden, When You Left Me

Chorus:
[My] brown-haired maiden, when
you left me
Not at all in fun with you
I went to [the copse?] yesterday
And that's the way we used to be.

4 When I saw you in the boat
It made my heart so sick and sore
When I saw you on the shore
My heart was more to grieve with
   you.

5 Many a night that I came home
Sitting down a while alone
Looking over at our home
And thinking of my dearest one.

6 ...fada bhuam
...ma thuath
 Rachainn choimhead air mo luaidh
 A dh'fhàg fo ghruaim 's fo
  mhìghean mi ?

6 ...far from me
...by north
I would go to see my love
Who left me sad and miserable.

7 Tha thu laghach tha thu còir
 Tha thu........

7 You are sweet and you are kind
 You are....

 .....
 .....

 .....
 .....

This was extremely popular at millings, as were other part-Gaelic/part-English (macaronic) songs, where everyone joined in the chorus, whether Gaelic-speaking or not. This is a composite version from Frank and Allan, sung on two separate occasions. Both had verses one to five, while only Allan had verses six and seven. Regrettably, the recording quality was marred by too many enthusiastic background noise-makers. The origin of the composition is a fascinating question—I assumed the song might only be found in the New World, but when I watched colleague Morag MacLeod's reaction of surprise as she recognized this as a song she had once heard during her childhood in Harris, we were left wondering if it had been brought back to the Old Country by one of the many Hebridean sailors who frequently visited Canada's Atlantic seaboard. Who knows?

Oran an Tombaca

Chorus:
Fal fal fal de re ro
Fal fal fal de rà
Fal e ré o fal de re o
Fal de re ro re ro rà.

1 'S binne leam na gogail coilich
   Moch a' ghoireadh anns an tom
   Torghan de bhotul ri gloine
   Agus duine thogas fonn.

2 Gur e mo ghaol an tombaca
   'S mór an tlachd a ghabhainn
      dhiot
   'S tric a chuir mi unnad tasdan
   Cha do chreach thu duine riamh.

3 Gur e bhuaidh a th'air an ruma
   Bheir e air duine bhith luath
   Bidh fear a' dannsa le chasan
   Bidh fear 's an leabaidh 'na
      shuain.

4 Huile fear nach bi rud aige
   Gur math leis gun tighinn gam
      chòir
   Nuair chi e mise 'ga chagnadh
   Cuiridh car tarsainn 'n a shròin.

5 'S iomadh mìle chuir mi riamh
      dhiom
   Cumail na fiachaill air dòigh
   Ach chan fhaighinn iad ro dheiseil
   Dar nach biodh esan nan còir.

6 Fàsaidh mi mar loman chosach
   Fàsaidh mi nam chrogan ruadh
   Fàgaidh modh mi agus maise
   Caillidh mi claisneachd mo
      chluas.

7 Falbhaidh mi sin dha na
      buithean
   Far am bi mo rùn air làmh
   Gu faighinn cairteal o Phenny
   Ged nach biodh teachd 'am an
      corr.

The Tobacco Song

Chorus:
Fal fal fal de re ro
Fal fal fal de ra
Fal e re o fal de re o
Fal de re ro re ro ra.

1 Sweeter to me than the clucking
      of a moorcock
   As it crows early on the hillock
   The sound of a bottle to a glass
   And a man who will sing a note.

2 The tobacco is my love
   And I greatly enjoy you
   Many a time I've spent a shilling
      on you
   But you've never robbed anyone.

3 The rum has quite an effect on
      one
   It makes one man run faster
   One dance with his feet
   And another in bed fast asleep.

4 Anyone who has nothing
   Would prefer not to come near me
   When he sees me chewing it
   He turns up his nose.

5 Many a mile I have travelled
   To keep my teeth satisfied
   But I didn't find them much use
   When it [the tobacco] wasn't
      between them.

6 I shall become like someone
      useless
   I shall become like a brown jar
   Manners and beauty will leave me
   I shall lose the hearing of my ears.

7 Then I'd go to the shops
   Where my love [tobacco] is at
      hand
   I can get a quarter from Penny
   Although I couldn't get [afford]
      any more.

This song which 'goes faster' was always reserved for the final stage of the work, when "the women knowed the cloth was milled—and it was hard to take it from them" they were enjoying the singing so much! They would smooth it out on the table for the final stage:

And then they would put it up in that roll, and then they had to sing a couple of songs after it was rolled, beating it down on this board.

That's a song that we generally use when we'd be through milling the cloth, we'd roll it up, and we would be slapping the cloth.' It's rolled up, you know, and stretched out and rolled up, and we used the song to slap it right down.... For that everybody would be slapping like this, their hands slapping the cloth, you know, beating it down, taking the wrinkles out of it. You'd have a spell on this side and then you'd turn it over and you'd do the other side. Well then, you'd do that twice, then it was okay.

And there's another name, now when the cloth 'd be all fixed up, then they'd get a piece of board about six inches wide and probably four feet long and they would roll it up. Now I don't know what they call it in English, you know, what we used to call it when the cloth was rolled up ready for... "ga chuir a choinneil."

And then you'd put it out in the sun to dry, you see, the next day and then it was fit for the old people to cut out clothes, whether it was a coat or a vest or pants.

The rolling songs (called "putting up songs" in Cape Breton) generally followed the songs known as *orain bassaidh* (clapping songs) where they occurred in Scotland. They were also of the chorus, verse, chorus pattern, but were sung at quicker tempo than the milling songs. These were also accompanied by laughter and lightheartedness, reflecting not only the theme of the songs but the pleasure of finishing the work, and the anticipation of the night of merry-making that would follow.

It is not surprising that Allan used the Gaelic phrase for this part of the procedure—"ga chuir a choinneil"—the same phrase had preceded the rolling of many a web of cloth in the MacArthur home as far back as he could remember. It is interesting to find the same phenomenon in the Scottish Hebrides, in a written account by the late Annie Johnston, "a gifted Barra lady who had an intimate knowledge of the Gaelic oral tradition of her native island." In her description translated from Gaelic she noted:

When the cloth was as thick as desired, the women then used to put it on the *coinneal*, that is, rolling it up in a roll, and singing an *oran basaidh*, clapping song. Clapping songs were usually light and funny, such as: 'Who will I take with me on the Irish ship?'[8]

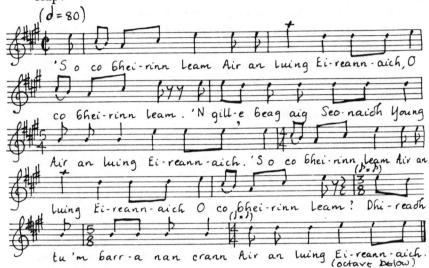

O CoBheirinn Leam	O Who Would I Take With Me
Chorus:	**Chorus:**
'S ó có bheirinn leam	And oh who would I take with me
Air an luing Eireannaich?	On the Irish ship
O có bheirinn leam?	Oh who would I take with me?

1 'N gille beag aig Seonaidh Young
   Air an luing Eireannaich
	1 Johnny Young's little boy
	   On the Irish ship

2 Dhìreadh tu 'm barra nan crann
   Air an luing Eireannaich
	2 You would climb to the top of
	   the mast
	   On the Irish ship

3 Theid e fodha 's ni e plum
   Air a ghrùnn éiridh e.
	3 He [the young lad] will go under
	   He will rise up from the bottom
	   and make a plonk.

Allan too had a version of this same song which he said he had not sung for many a long year.

This song, which Allan referred to as "only a kind of a rhyme, you know," was generally thought of in Scotland as a matchmaking song to be sung at the end of a waulking. The women would have a bit of sport with each other, playfully teasing individuals by naming a man who would be known to everyone, as is described by Francis Tolmie who collected it in Skye in 1900.

There is scope for the leader to improvise teasing and nonsensical verses. One of these is An Long Eireannach, dated to [collected it in] 1900. "Ho!" runs the chorus, "whom shall I take with me on board the Irish ship? Is it Donald I will take, and we shall go far under sail." The leader would continue, coupling the name of Donald—or Peter, Alastair or John, as might be—with that of one of the women, elderly or young, who was eventually supposed to rescue him from a pummelling in the folds of the cloth, or from the tub into which he had fallen—he is being treated as if he were the web of cloth—before bearing him off on the imaginary Irish ship.[9]

When the actual work of the evening was over, the roll of cloth and the boards were cleared away. The women took off their aprons and people who wished to do so quickly washed and tidied themselves in preparation for the ceilidh that followed. The hostess set the table with a prepared feast of their own roast pork or chicken, homegrown potatoes, carrots and turnips, along with pickles, a variety of preserved local berries, homebaked breads, *bonnoch* and cakes. The host, in the meantime, offered a glass to everyone— whisky, rum, homemade beer, wine, or moonshine.

Oran an t-Saighdear	***The Soldier's Song***
Chorus:	Chorus:
Hù a hó tha mi fo liondubh	Hu a ho I am under sadness
Hug órann ó mi trom gu dìreadh	Hug oran o I'm heavy [hearted]
Hù a hó tha mi fo liondubh.	climbing [a hill]
	Hu a ho I am sad.

1 'N oidhche bha mi aig a'
    mhuileann
  Thruis a' chuideachda mu'm
    thimcheall.

2 Chuir iad an t-òr dearg nam
    phòca
  Chan e mo thoir bhith 'ga innse.

3 Chuir iad an it' àrd 'nam
    bhoineid
  Bha siod dorranach le m'
    mhuinntir.

4 Thoir mo shoraidh-sa gum
    mhàthair
  Bho 's i 's cràiteach dh'fhàg mi'n
    tìr sin.

5 Dìreadh ris a' charra chreagain
  Tha mise 'n eagal nach till sinn.

6 Dìreadh ris na Beanna Siùbhrach
  Donnchadh Bàn 's a chùl ri
    dhìlsean.

1 The night I was at the mill
  The company gathered around
    me.

2 They put the red gold in my
    pocket
  I am ashamed to tell it.

3 They put the tall feather in my
    cap
  And that was difficult for my
    people.

4 Take my blessing to my mother
  Since she is the saddest one I left
    in that place.

5 Climbing the craggy hill
  I'm afraid we won't return.

6 Climbing the hills of Jura
  Duncan Ban [fair] has left
    behind his loved ones.

The rest of the evening (which continued well into the night) was spent eating, drinking, singing, playing music, and dancing. The countless tunes and songs heard in one evening could well fill their own volumes, but the remaining songs which are included here are those which Allan sang as a typical contribution to any ceilidh.

In Scotland, you know, in the wars at that time, the Black Watch, Reisimeid Dhubh... well, you had to be over six feet or else you wouldn't be taken in the Black Watch at that time in Scotland. They were going... they were pressing them you know, you *had* to go—the people in Scotland—for the Black Watch; when they come around you had to go. They would examine you and if you were the height and everything, you were physical fit, you know, well there was no getting out of it. They used to call *racruitear*. I don't know what they calls it in English. [Recruiters, as in recruiting sergeants.]

Although this song does not appear in recorded or printed collections that I know in Scotland, there is a Cape Breton variant in John Shaw's unpublished collection.

Dean Cadalan Sàmhach

Chorus:

Dean cadalan sàmhach a chuilein
 's a rùin
Fuirich mar tha thu 's thu 'n
 dràsd' an ait ùr
Tha òganaich againn làn
 bheairteas is chliù
Bidh tusa 'na d' oighre air fear
 eiginn dhiùbh.

1 'Sann an Ameiriga tha sinn an
 dràsd'
Fo dhubhar na coille nach teirig
 gu bràth
Dar dh'fhalbhas an Dùldach 's a
 thionndaidh's am barr
Bidh measan 's bidh ùbhlan gu
 dlùtharr a' fàs.

2 Is truagh nach robh mise ann an
 dùthaich Mhicleoid
Far an d'fhuair mi òg m'àrach 'n
 am phàisde glé òg
.....
.....

Sleep Peacefully

Chorus:

Sleep peacefully, my pet, my love
Stay as you are, and you being in
 a new place
We have young men full of riches
 and renown
And you will be the heir to one or
 other of them.

1 It's in America that you are now
Under the shade of the wood
 that goes on without end
When the winter goes away and
 the crops change colour
Berries and apples will be
 growing in abundance.

2 Would that I were in the land of
 MacLeod
Where I was reared as a very
 young child
.....
.....

At any ceilidh you could expect to find one or more nursing mothers in the company. Babies were warmly welcomed, and much attention paid to them. The customs surrounding the care of infants and small children in the Codroy Valley are identical to the pattern found in the Highlands and Islands of Scotland where it is virtually unheard of to 'abandon' a baby in a cot or cradle without singing and rocking it to sleep. Lullabies are part of the repertoire of every parent and grandparent, and the rocking chair a part of the furnishings. Allan's mother was as typical as any:

> Oh, indeed, she used to take them on her knee and nurse them and sing them to sleep. And when the baby would be about three weeks old and she'd go out in the burnt ground and she'd make a little place for the baby alongside of a stump and cover him up and feed him and she'd go on planting potatoes. You won't find women today doing that!

In those days there were relatively few years between singing to one's own children and to grandchildren, as families were generally large, and as Allan MacArthur recalled with certain mirth, childbearing years were not restricted as they tend to be today. "Oh well, she had a baby when she was fifty! Of course, she was from the old stock!"

This song, which has many versions, was composed by the eighteenth century poet John MacRae, or Iain mac Mhurchaidh, as he is known in Gaelic. He grew up in Kintail, which is very close to the area that Allan's grandmother came from, and in 1774 he emigrated to North Carolina where he composed this and other songs. It is known that his American compositions were brought back to Scotland by a man who emigrated with Iain mac Mhurchaidh, so one might surmise that Allan's people heard it in their native Moidart before their emigration. Allan's tune is a variant of one sung in Scotland.

Gràin na Caillich

Chorus:

O hì o hà gur cruaidh a' chailleach
O hì o hà gur fuar a' chailleach
Ho rì ho rà 's e gràin na caillich
Dh'fhàg mise 'n am amadan
  gòrrach.

1 Ma theid mi'n taigh-osd' 's an
    stòp a cheannach
  No suidhe aig bòrd 's gun òlainn
    drama
  Theid fàileadh na sròin bidh
    dòrn a' tarraig
  Bidh muinntir a' bhaile ri mòd
    orm.

2 Mar ceannaich mi'n "tea" cha
    d'fhiach mi'n earraid
  A' leagadh a cinn 's i tinn a'
    gearain
  Cha dean i rium sìth ach strì is
    carraid
  'S i cnàmhan teallaich an
    còmhuidh.

3 Nuair thig mi bho'n chrann an
    am an earraich
  Bidh fuachd air mo chàil 's mi'n
    geall mo gharadh
  Cha'n fhaod mi' na taing dhol
    teann air an teallach
  Mu'm buail i gu h-ealamh le
    bròig mi.

4 Cha dean i dhomh feum 's cha
    ghréidh i aran
  Cha'n aithnich i fuaghal spréidh
    no leanabh
  A' laighe 's ag éirigh 's ag
    éigheach 's a' gearain
  'S gun creicinn gu deimhinn air
    gròt i.

5 Gun fiacaill 'na ceann 's car cam
    na peirceall
  Nuair thogadh i greann an am an
    fheasgair

Disgust at the Old Woman

Chorus:

O hi o ha, hard is the old woman
O hi o ha, cold is the old woman
Ho ri ho ra, I'm disgusted with
  the old woman
Who left me a stupid fool.

1 If I go to an inn to buy a stoup
    of liquor
  Or sit at the table to drink a dram
  The smell of it goes up her nose
    and she shakes her fist
  And the people of the town will
    be talking about me
  [literally, passing judgement on
  me].

2 If I don't buy tea, I'm no use
  She'd be hanging her head, sick
    and complaining
  She won't make peace with me,
    but argues and opposes
  And she's forever grumbling.

3 When I come from the plough in
    spring
  I'm cold right through, and
    looking forward to
    getting warmed
  I'm not allowed to get anywhere
    near the hearth
  In case she gives me a swift kick
    with her boot.

4 She won't do any work and she
    won't make bread
  She won't raise livestock, cattle
    or a baby
  Going to bed and getting up
  [she's] shouting and moaning
  I could gladly sell her for a groat
    [Scots coin].

5 Without a tooth in her head and
    a crooked twist in her jaw
  When she grinned angrily in the
    evening

Gun teicheadh gach crann, gach
clann 's gach seisreach
Le mheud 's a bha dh'eagal o
ghròigeas.

Every plough, every child, every
ploughteam fleed from her
So great was their fear of her
surliness.

"And the one that composed that, you know, he was never married. He never had a wife, although he composed the song!"

"And the song was composed in Scotland. He was never married, although he gave the poor woman such a calling down!"

Allan informed me that the bard who composed this song about two hundred years ago was Allan MacDougall, or Ailean Dall (Blind Allan) originally of Glencoe. During the latter half of his life, he was the family bard to MacDonald of Glengarry, where the Codroy Valley MacIsaacs came from, and, as Allan MacArthur pointed out, "You can read his life story yourself in *Sàr Obair*, starting on page 298!"

Will You Marry Me My Bonnie Fair Lassie

Chorus:
Will you marry me, my bonnie
fair lassie?
Will you marry me, my damsel?
Answer me my bonnie fair lassie
'S fhad a bha mi fhin is mi 'n geall
ort.

1 Car do Niall Mhac Guair thu,
e fhéin 's an ?t-aghan ruadh?
Ghabh iad suas 'sa' bhruach 's e
tighinn
teann air....?
Fhuair e suas air ghualainn, rug e
'n sin air chluais air

Will you Marry me, My Bonnie Fair Lassie

Chorus:
Will you marry me, my bonnie
fair lassie
Will you marry me, my damsel?
Answer me my bonnie fair lassie
It's a long time since we were
pledged to each other.

1 You're a relative of Neil
MacQuarry, himself and
the little red ?heifer
They went up the brae and he was
getting near? it
He got it by the shoulder, then
he grabbed him by the ear
Whalloping you on the head
with a stick.

Maid' aige ga bhualadh man cheann ort.

2 Mi fhéin is Iain Dhòmhaill 'sa' mhaduinn moch Di-Dòmhnaich
Léine bheag gheal agus "tie" orainn
Ar dosain air a lìobadh 's ar smig air an sgrìobadh
A' falbh chon na gruagaich 's na *Highlands*.

3 Coimhead thusa 'n dràsda air Mìcheal Iain Bhàin
Buideal aige làn is dà cheann ann
Ma théid thu dhan àite 's a chuireas tu air fàilte
Glainne bheag 'na làimh bheir e dram dhut.

2 Myself and Donald's Iain [Iain, son of Donald] on Sunday morning
Wearing a little white shirt and with our ties on
Our hair sleeked and our chins shaven
Going to see the maiden in the Highlands.

3 Look now at Fair John's Michael
He has a full cask quite unopened
If you go to his place, and greet him
He'll have a small glass in his hand and will give you a dram.

This song is another composition by Allan's brother, Murdoch who lived further up the Valley at Highlands. The entire room of people could join in the chorus, regardless of whether they spoke Gaelic or not.

Air Fàillirin Illirin Uillirin ó

Chorus:
Air fàillirin ìllirin ùillirin ó
Air fàillirin ìllirin ùillirin ó
Air fàillirin ìllirin ùillirin ó
Gur bòidheach an comunn th'aig coinneamh 'n t-Strath-mhóir.

1. Not the swan on the lake or the foam on the shore
   Can compare with the charms of the maid I adore;
   Not so white is the new milk that flows o'er the pail
   Or the snow that is showered from the boughs of the vale.

2 Gur gile no leannan na 'n eal' air an t-snàmh
   Na cobhar na tuinne 's e tilleadh bho'n tràigh
   Na'm blàth-bhainne buaile 's a chuach leis fo bhàrr,
   Na sneachd nan gleann dosrach 'ga fhroiseadh mu'n bhlàr.

3. Tha cas-fhalt mo rùin-sa gu siùbhlach a snìomh,
   Mar na neòil bhuidhe lùbas air stùcaibh nan sliabh
   Tha gruaidh mar an ròs 'nuair a's bòidhche bhios fhiamh
   Fo ùr-dhealt a' Chéitein mun éirich a' ghrian.

4. The mavis and lark when they welcome the dawn
   Make a chorus of joy to resound through the morn
   But the mavis is tuneless, the lark strives in vain
   When my beautiful charmer renews her sweet strain.

This is part of the Gaelic song "Ealaidh Ghaoil" by Ewen MacLachlan, contained in *Sàr Obair*, with English verse translation by the composer. On the occasion the song was recorded, Allan began by singing the English verse translation of "Gur gile mo leannan...," then went straight to the second Gaelic verse which he later showed me in *Sàr Obair*, translated as follows:

As the cloud's yellow wreath on the mountain's high brow.
The locks of my fair one abundantly flow;
 Her cheeks have the tint that the roses display,
When they glitter with dew on the morning of May.

Although he sang no Gaelic equivalent to his final verse, I feel sure that Allan would wish to give the Gaelic reader the same consideration as I would by including it here:

Bidh 'n uiseag 's an smeòrach feadh lòintean nan driuchd,
'Toirt fàilte le'n òrain do'n òg-mhadainn chiùin
Ach tha'n uiseag neo-sheòlta 's an smeòrach gun sunnd,
'Nuair thòisicheas m'eudail air gleusadh a ciùil.

The life story of Ewan MacLachlan (1775-1822), the Lochaber bard who composed this song, was of great fascination to Allan MacArthur who referred to *Sàr Obair* for his information. Considering the facts that MacLachlan translated the first seven books of Homer's *Illiad* from Greek into Gaelic heroic verse, and was not only a bard but also a renowned scholar of both Classics and Celtic, we might well share Allan's respect!

While there appears to be nobody in the Valley today who sings the above English words to this tune, there is yet another set of words Allan had which kept it very much alive, namely "The Dominion Mine Strike Song."

The Dominion Mine Strike Song
[to the tune of the above song]

Chorus:
Air fàillirin ìllirin ùillirin ó
Air fàillirin ìllirin ùillirin ó
Air fàillirin ìllirin ùillirin ó
There's policemen and soldiers wherever you go.

1 Come all you young fellows who knew friends of mine,
You'll always remember the year nineteen-nine.
A dirtier crowd you could never find
And those who were scabbing were down in the mine.

2 The strike it began in the morning so dark,
To see those poor fellows would break a man's heart,
Parading the streets in their badges so bright.
And mind you those fellows they think they're all right.

3 That day at Dominion the strike it did start,
The Mayor and the Council they thought they were smart,
They called on the soldiers with cannons and lead,
And doctors and nurses looked after the dead.

4 There's a cop from Loch Lomond who walks a big track,
And if you go near him he'll leap on your back;
There's old Martin Heally and Johnny MacLeod,
And to see those poor fellows would make a man proud.

5 There's Mr. George Dunfy, I nearly forgot,
He's neither an official nor is he a cop.
From living life hard and from suffering from piles,
He's now just as thin as a three-cornered file!

6 Success to John Luscombe, I wish him good luck
He's the only town father that had any pluck.
When the Mayor and the Council they thought us to kill,
Well he fought and he fought, and he'll fight for us still.

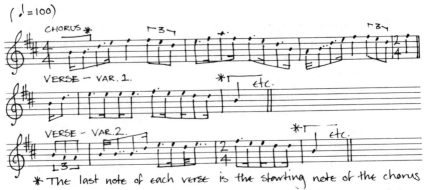

*The last note of each verse is the starting note of the chorus

[musical notation is approximate as the tape recording was so drowned out by the noise of the milling]

Air faill ill eile hu a go

Chorus:
Air faill ill éile hù a gó
Hi iù a hó nam b'fhearr leat mi
Air faill ill éile hù a gó

1 ...ghillean òga
...nach do phàigh i e.

2 On a chuir thu suas an currac
...a dh'fhàg thu mi

3 Cuir am botul air a' bhòrd
'Se seo na seòid a thràigheadh e.

4 Dùileam gur e clachan daoimean
Bha *shine* adh 's na stràidean ann.

5 Dùileam gur e clachan siùcair
Bha dùnadh nan gàrraidhean.

6 Gur e nighean Dho'ill ac Dhòmhaill
An ribhinn òg a ràghnaich mi.

7 Dar a chuir i suas an currac
'S muladach a dh'fhàg i mi.

Air faill ill eile hu a go

Chorus:
Air faill ill eile hu a go
Hi iu a ho if you preferred me
Air faill ill eile hu a go.

1 ...young boys (youths)
...she didn't pay it.

2 Since you put on the bonnet
...and you left me.

3 Put the bottle on the table
We are the lads who'd drain it.

4 I thought it was stones of diamonds
That were shining in the streets.

5 [Then] I thought it was stones of sugar
That were closing up the garden wall.

6 It was the daughter of Donald MacDonald
Who was the young girl that I had chosen.

7 When she put her bonnet on
She left me very sad.

Allan sang this song with Sandy MacIsaac and his two brothers, Hector and Archie. Although the three men were considerably older than the lads who may have originally sung this drinking song, the setting was as it may have been in the original context of the song—"bha botul ruma air a bhòrd" (There was a bottle of rum on the table) and a fair amount of noise and laughter in the background.

Unfortunately, some of the words were drowned out by the noise, and I never had another opportunity to ask any of the men about this song. Possibly composed in Canada (John Shaw has collected a Cape Breton variant), it obviously dates to the time when the *currac* (frilled bonnet or *mutch*) signified the married state of women. The custom that prevailed in some areas of Scotland till early this century was that young unmarried women wore a *stìomag* (snood) which, after marriage, was exchanged for a mutch. No doubt the images of the song tell of a young man whose beloved, "nighean Do'ill ac Dhòmhnaill," married someone else, and he resorts to the oblivion of the bottle.

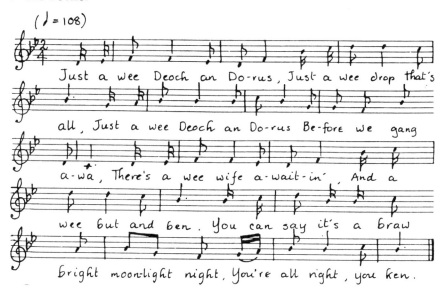

(♩ = 108)

Just a wee Deoch an Do-rus, Just a wee drop that's all, Just a wee Deoch an Do-rus Be-fore we gang a-wa, There's a wee wife a-wait-in', And a wee but and ben. You can say it's a braw bright moon-light night, You're all right, you ken.

Just a Wee Deoch an Dorus

Chorus:
Just a wee Deoch an Dorus
Just a wee drop that's all
Just a wee Deoch an Dorus
Before we gang awa
There's a wee wife awaitin'
A wee but and ben
You can say it's a braw bright moonlight night
You're all right, you ken.[10]

1 There a good old Scottish custom
That has stood the test of time
It's a custom that is carried out
In every land and clime
Where brother Scots foregather

It's all the usual thing
And just for old acquaintance sake
We'll all unite and sing.

2 I like a man that is a man
A man that's straight and fair
The sort of man that will and can
In all things do his share
I like a man, a jolly man
The sort of man you know
The chap that slaps you on the back
Here Jock before we go.

3 I'll invite you all some other night
To come and bring your pipe
I'll promise you the grandest time
You had in all your life
We'll have the bagpipes calling
We'll dance the Highland Fling
And just for old acquaintance sake
We'll all unite and sing.

The advent of radio and gramophone added many songs to the repertoires of all singers, including the above Harry Lauder song which remains popular to the present time.

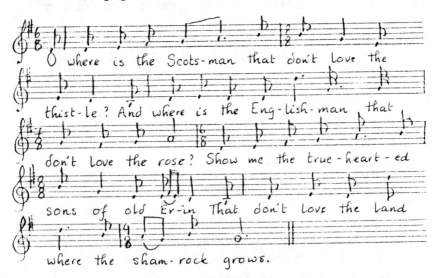

O where is the Scots-man that don't love the thist-le? And where is the Eng-lish-man that don't love the rose? Show me the true-heart-ed sons of old Er-in That don't love the land where the sham-rock grows.

The Shamrock, Thistle and Rose

Chorus:
O where is the Scotsman that don't love the thistle?
And where is the Englishman that don't love the rose?

Show me the true-hearted sons of old Erin
That don't love the land where the shamrock grows.

1 The English they boast of their glorious Nelson
    And well they may boast of such men
    For they met and defeated the fleets at Trafalgar
    And fought on, the brave English boys.

2 The Irish they boast of the... of Evans
    O'Donnell and Brian Boru
    Well they worked hard....
    .....

3 The Scotsmen they boast of their Bruce and their Wallace
    And well they may boast of such men
    For they proved themself true to the thistle and heather
    Their equals they'll never find again.

4 And long may the English, the Irish and Scotsmen
    United defy all their foes
    And long may they live to possess those dear emblems
    The shamrock, thistle and rose.

At the ceilidh at Sandy MacIsaac's house in St. Andrews, Allan was enthusiastically requested to sing "Shamrock, Thistle and Rose" by several people present. His own comment that it tells of "when England and France was so hard against one another" gives no hint of where it was composed, or when. It's theme of patriotism is reminiscent of the song "The Irish Colleen."[11] As yet I have found no comparative song outside the Codroy Valley, but it has a ring about it which suggests to me the 1920s Boston music-hall tradition.

Rolling Home

Chorus:
Rolling home, rolling home.
Rolling home across the sea,

Rolling home to Bonnie Scotland
Rolling home dear land to thee.

1 Twice a thousand miles behind us
   And a thousand miles before
   Ancient ocean seems to bear us
   On that well-remembered shore.

2 And the wild waves left behind us
   Seem to murmur as they flow
   There are kindly hearts awaiting
   In the land to which we go.

Allan sang a more complete version of this sea-shanty while out for a drive one day; he also sang "What Shall We Do With The Drunken Sailor." But as driver and listener I could not record it. The above fragment is from Frank's singing, with a rousing family chorus in the background. While the song has many versions (Rolling Home to Dear Old England; ...to Caledonia; ...Dear Old Hamburg) the melody which the MacArthurs sang is distinctively different to the well-known melody popular in Scotland.[12]

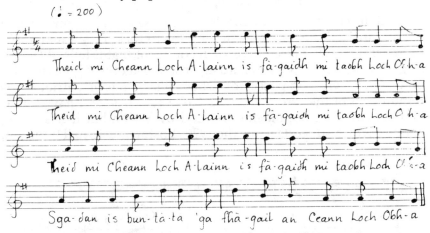

Theid mi Cheann Loch Alainn	**I Will Go to Kinlochaline**

Theid mi Cheann Loch Alainn is
   fàgaidh mi taobh Loch Obha
	I will go to Kinochaline and
	   I will leave the side of Loch Awe

Theid mi Cheann Loch Alainn is
   fàgaidh mi taobh Loch Obha
	I will go to Kinochaline and
	   I will leave the side of Loch Awe

Theid mi Cheann Loch Alainn	I will go to Kinochaline and
Is fàgaidh mi taobh Loch Obha	I will leave the side of Loch Awe
Sgadan is buntata 'ga fhàgail	There's herring and potatoes to be
an Ceann Loch Obha.	left at the head of Loch Awe.

This *pruit* is immediately recognizable to pipers as the reel "The Smith of Chillichassie"—not the easiest of tunes to play, they'll tell you, but as Allan pointed out, "it goes a lot easier on your fingers when you knows the words of it." He was quick to teach his catchy tunes with their tricky, light-hearted words, such as the above or (to give but one more example), this short rhythmic ditty, to the tune "Cock of the North":

> Cuiridh Iain Dhòmhaill sìos an inneir
> 'S cuiridh e suas buntàta.
>
> John son of Donald will put manure down
> And it will send up the potatoes.

These are only two of several dance tunes which were popularly sung and which are still played on accordion and fiddle. Though the fiddle was the most popular instrument for step-dancing, there was an added excitement when a singer or two provided the music:

> And when the cloth was milled, they'd put everything away and start dancing. There would be no waltzes [except old-fashioned waltzes] or jazz, or anything—all step-dancing. We'd have an eight-handed reel, you see, or a set, or something like that, but only eight—that was the highest [number of people] that would go on the floor at one time. But for step-dancing, there was only four people on the floor—two men and two women. And they'd beat you down!
>
> It's different kinds of dances altogether now, you see. There'd be as high as fifty or sixty get up for a dance now. That's quite different to when they'd be only four on the floor, and everybody trying to see who could dance the best, who could dance the most steps.

So often during the recording sessions the spontaneity of the enthusiastic company added to the atmosphere to such an extent that several songs have indistinct words, impossible to transcribe for this collection. It may well be that someone somewhere can fill in the blanks of these untranscribed lines. It was certainly my own earnest intention to go back over them with the only authority I knew on the subject—Allan MacArthur. Sadly, however, the summer he sang them was to be the last one he enjoyed reasonable health. By the following September he had gone. To quote the archaic words he himself showed me in his beloved *Sàr Obair*, in the biography of the bard Ailean Dall (Allan MacDougall): "But alas! The book was only in progress when the cold finger of death silenced his harp for ever. He died much regretted...." In Allan MacArthur's case, he passed away on September 10, 1971, and there is no doubt that the loss of the personality was placed far above the loss of his unique songs.

Postscript

> Bho'n chaill mi Ghàidhlig na b'fhearr cha
> d'fhuair mi.
> Since I've lost the Gaelic language, nothing
> better have I found.
> *A Gaelic Proverb from Allan MacArthur*

There may well be few books written in the 1980s about the Scots overseas which do not mention the tartan as an identifiable part of Scottish tradition. It is, after all, the one thing which Scots the world over can proudly wear as a badge of identity, instantly recognizable and without a word spoken, it will make them stand out as being definitely Scottish.

To Allan MacArthur's generation and those that preceded his time, the real identity lay in something much deeper. Certainly they admired the tartan! The *Reisimeid Dhubh* (Black Watch) look magnificent in it, and the Scots Guards too! And the pipe bands... how they would love to see one in the Valley! But the idea of those splendid colours as the main identity was something to question. Just as the Highlanders and Islanders who remained behind in the Old Country could not regard the modest contents of their wardrobe, homespun and often drab, as setting them apart from other cultures, so too was the attitude of the Scottish Newfoundlanders. The real identity was in the fabric of the people themselves: their language, their lore, their lifestyle, all woven into the very essence of their individuality. Most important of all to Allan's generation was the mother tongue. They realized only too well that the Gaelic language had been the vehicle for carrying their Scottish traditions from one generation to the next. With its rapid decline, the traditions it upheld would be forced to follow.

Allan's son, Frank, summed up the situation well when he noted his own generation as a turning point:

> I used to find it so funny when I started going over there [the MacArthur family homestead] first and everybody in the house could speak Gaelic, but still they'd be speaking English. But after a while I fell the same way, we'd all kinda speak English.... But if I went over home and he [Allan] was outside, or something, we'd still speak Gaelic, you know. Well, I don't know why they turned to English. I don't know.
>
> Nowadays I have to hesitate with a lot of words, you know, if I got into a conversation on.... I would have to stop and think, whereas probably fifty years ago it would be just like running downhill. No problem! But with practice I'd get it back no problem. I'm sure it would be a matter of a week and I'd be back the same as I was when I was a little boy.

Frank observed that the generations that preceded his own were thoroughly Gaelic; his own generation stood at a turning point, where they were fluent in Gaelic but through intermarriage and increased influence from outside communication, they were obliged to use English; and the generations which follow are totally English-speaking.

That is not to say, however, that the Scottish Newfoundlanders cannot still be easily identified. (The Scottish Highlands and Islands are suffering a similar fate, with thousands of their people unable to speak the language, yet still retaining many characteristics of the Gael.) Their manner of speech, certain aspects of their lifestyle, and certainly their music clearly indicate a strong Scottish Highland background. The ceilidh may have changed in many respects, but it is still very much alive in the Codroy Valley, a product of generations of Gaelic tradition.

During the past fifteen years there has been a revival of interest in the traditions of the Codroy Valley people of all backgrounds. Mary MacArthur saw the small beginnings of it after the death of her husband, and in her own way she greatly contributed by encouraging the preservation of the Scottish traditions. To begin with, she spent many hours either across her own kitchen table, or via letter, carefully going over my original manuscript, adding interesting comment, making me more aware of certain aspects of their way of life. Furthermore, she showed delight and approval when several members of the community agreed to take part in the Folk Arts Council competitions in the early 1970s. It marked the beginning of a series of successes, after which the Codroy Valley people gained recognition not only across Newfoundland but further afield: Frank MacArthur won the All-Newfoundland step-dancing competition; his nephew, Leonard, was the top fiddler; his brother, Sears, was runner-up to the Newfoundland accordion champion; and a group of eight square-dancers from the Valley, accompanied by Sears, won the square-dancing. It was a proud day for Mrs. MacArthur when they returned to the Valley, not only with the honours of winning but with a revitalized pride in their Scottish heritage. "If only Allan could have seen them," she commented, "wouldn't he be some proud!" Before her death on January 10, 1975, Mary MacArthur gave me the same quiet assurance that she, like her husband before her, was happy to know that some of their traditions were recorded for future generations who may develop an interest in their forebears.

Regrettably, neither one lived long enough to see the completed work which is, in reality, their story. Nor did they have the pleasure in knowing that the creativity that had produced singers and song-makers in the past had lived on to the present generation of their own grandchildren. Two of them in particular, Loretta and Gordon Cormier (children of Margaret [nee MacArthur] and Leo Cormier) have made a distinguished contribution to music in the Codroy Valley, and have extended their talent to many parts of Canada and the United States. Certainly they sing and play in a wide range of music and song—much of their repertoire incorporates modern trends popularized by the media; some of it includes Newfoundland-Irish jigs and reels, but distinctively Scottish; and found nowhere else in Newfoundland are the strathspeys and reels such as "Calum Crubach" and "Muileann Dubh" and the Gaelic waltzes such as "Cailin Mo Ruinsa" or "Morag a Dunbheagain." If you were to afford yourself the summer pleasure of attending the Codroy Valley Folk Festival (another product of the revival) you would see and hear a splendid array of local singers, musicians, and dancers who would leave you in no doubt that the Scottish traditions are still clearly discernible.

Great would have been the joy of Mary and Allan MacArthur to know that the people of the Codroy Valley had indeed developed a new and vital interest in the music and culture which had been their own greatest source of pride throughout their lives. Allan's favourite toast is as apt today as it was when he first heard it:

> *Deoch slàinte chuairtear a ghluais bho Albainn!*
> *Here's a health to the traveller that left Scotland!*

Notes

Introduction

[1]Harold Horwood, *Newfoundland* (Toronto: MacMillan, 1969), p.20.

[2]Philip D. Jordan, "The Folklorist as a Social Historian," in *Western Folklore*, XII, 3 (July 1953), 194- 201.

[3]W. Lynwood Montell, *The Saga of Coe Ridge: A Study in Oral History* (Knoxville: University of Tennessee Press, 1970), p. xx.

[4]*Ibid.*, p. 195.

[5]All tapes are housed in Memorial University of Newfoundland Folklore Archives.

Chapter 1

[1]W. Prowse (ed.), *The Newfoundland Guide Book* (London: 1895; 3rd ed. 1911), pp. 78-79, 178. Although the sketch maps do not accurately represent the coastal outline of the area, they show detail of the names of the best fishing pools used locally.

Chapter 2

[1]J.B. Jukes, *Excursions in and about Newfoundland During the Years 1839 and 1840*, 2 vols (London: J. Murray, 1842), vol. 1, p. 172. Hereafter cited as *Excursions*

[2]*Ibid.*, vol. 1, p. 173.

[3]William Epps Cormack, *Narrative of a Journey Across the Island of Newfoundland in 1822*, 2nd ed. (London, New York & Toronto: Longman, Green and Co., 1928), pp. 91-92. Hereafter cited as *Narrative*.

[4]*Ibid.*, p. 105.

[5]*Ibid.*, pp. 99-100.

[6]Archdeacon Edward Wix, *Six Months of a Newfoundland Missionary's Journal, from February to August 1835* (London: 1836), p. 127. Hereafter cited as *Journal*.

[7]*Ibid.*, p. 135.

[8]I can find no reference which would ascertain who first imported cattle, when it was, or from where the cattle were imported.

[9]Wix, *Journal*, p. 135.

[10]Jukes, *Excursions.*, vol. 1, p. 176.

[11]*Ibid.*

[12]Unfortunately, some of the St. Anne's parish records were lost in a fire which consumed the Searston church in 1930 after a lighting storm. Although those records which were kept in the priest's house were saved, Father R. White said that there was "no telling" what those housed in the old church might have contained.

[13]Rev. Michael Brosnan, *Pioneer History of the Parish of St. Georges* (Toronto: Mission Press, 1948), p. 13. Hereafter cited as *Pioneer History*.

[14]John Lorne Campbell, *Canna: The Story of a Hebridean Island* (Oxford: 1984), pp. 152-53.

[15]*Ibid.*, p. 162.

[16]Letter from John Lorne Campbell to author, 21 November 1986.

[17]*Ibid.*

[18]*Ibid.*, pp. 249-51.

[19]Mary L. Fraser, *Folklore of Nova Scotia* (n.p., n.d.), p. 8.

[20]Nova Scotia did not, in fact, make the final decision to join Canada until 1867.

[21]Rev. Charles MacDonald, *Moidart; or Among the Clanranalds* (Oban: Cameron, 1889), pp. 171-74.

[22]*Ibid.*, p. 11.

[23]Julie Morris, *Tracing Your Ancestors in Nova Scotia* (Halifax: Public Archives of Nova Scotia), p. 11.

[24]Hilda Chaulk Murray's excellent book *More Than 50%* (St. John's: Breakwater Books, 1979) affirms that this was certainly accepted in early Newfoundland outports.

[25]Thomas Sears, *Report of the Missions Prefecture Apostolic Western Newfoundland* (n.p., 1877), pp. 21-22.

[26]Brosnan, *Pioneer History.*, p. 15.

[27]*Ibid.*

[28]Letter from Father Thomas Sears to Rt. Rev. J.T. Mullock, Bishop of St. John's, in The *Newfoundlander* (St. John's), No. 6554, 18 December 1868.

[29]Thomas Sears, *Report of the Missions*, p. 28.

[30]Jukes, *Excursions*, vol. 1, p. 12.

31Brosnan, *Pioneer History*, p. 78.

[32]Letter from Sears to Mullock.

[33]To date, unfortunately, I have been unable to find an account in the *Journals of the House of Assembly of Newfoundland* of the procedure carried out for this election or the names of those elected. There are, however, numerous references to the district in which the Codroy Valley was

represented along with reports of petitions made to the government and the progress made in the area.

[34]*Journal of the House of Assembly of Newfoundland*, 1884, Appendix, p. 512. Hereafter cited as *JHA*.

[35]Mr. Boone in the House of Assembly, 19 April 1834.

[36]Brosnan, *Pioneer History*, p. 78.

Chapter 3

[1]Alexander MacDonald, *Story and Song from Loch Ness- Side* (Inverness: 1914), p. 207.

[2]D.S. Thompson, "The Gaelic Oral Tradition," *Proceedings of the Scottish Anthropological and Folklore Society*, 5: 1-17 (1954), 3.

[3]Kenneth Jackson, "Folktale in Gaelic Scotland," *Proceedings of the Scottish Anthropological and Folklore Society*, Vol. IV, No. 3 (1952), pp. 123-36.

[4]*Ibid.*, p. 137.

[5]John MacKenzie, *Sar-Obair nam Bard Gaelach: The Beauties of Gaelic Poetry and Lives of the Highland Bards* (Halifax: 1863).

[6]Charles W. Dunn, *Highland Settler: A Portrait of the Scottish Gael in Nova Scotia* (Toronto: University of Toronto Press, 1953), pp. 49-50. Hereafter cited as *Highland Settler*.

[7]On first hearing the words "what we call Corner Brook or Bay of Islands," I was under the impression that Allan MacArthur thought that I had never heard of the well-known west coast town of Corner Brook. Later, I realized that this was only another example of his desire to be accurate, for in the days of which he spoke there was no place in the Bay of Islands called Corner Brook, as that town only came into existence in 1923.

[8]Dunn, *Highland Settler*, p. 45.

[9]"Here's a health to the traveller who left Scotland!" This line is also the first of a song in "The Emigrant Experience" by Sister Margaret MacDonell (Toronto: 1980).

Chapter 4

[1]Allan's "recipe for coffee" was certainly known in Scotland. This is affirmed by a School of Scottish Studies recording from South Uist in 1970 from D.A. Johnson who described the same process using barley bread.

Chapter 5

[1]There is slight variation in the dates of celebrating the Twelve Days, not only within Newfoundland but also within Great Britain.

[2]Although *bonnach* was a staple food of the Scots eaten all year round, there was a time when Christmas Eve (or Yule E'en) was called *Oidhche nam Bannag*, Night of the Bannocks. Mary MacLeod Banks, *British Calendar Customs: Scotland*, 3 vols. (London and Glasgow: Folk Lore Society, 1941), vol. 3, pp. 202-06.

[3]Borrowing from English words which did not exist in the Gaelic is discussed by Charles W. Dunn in *Highland Settler*, pp. 142-44.

[4]John F. Szwed, "The Mask of Friendship: Mummering as a Ritual of Social Relations," in Herbert Halpert and George M. Story (eds.), *Christmas Mumming in Newfoundland* (Toronto: University of Toronto Press, 1969), pp. 104-18.

[5]*Ibid.*, p. 113.

[6]For a few Scottish examples, see John Gregorson Campbell, *Witchcraft and Second Sight in the Highlands and Islands of Scotland* (Glasgow: J. MacLehose and Sons, 1902), pp. 230-36. Hereafter cited as *Witchcraft and Second Sight*. See also, Alexander Carmichael (trans. & ed.), *Carmina Gadelica*, 5 vols. (Edinburgh and London: Oliver and Boyd, 1928-54), vol. 1, p. 148. For a few examples from the New World, and from Cape Breton in particular, see *Cape Breton's Magazine* Number 2 (Skir Dhu: 1973), p. 2, and Dunn, *Highland Settler*, p. 51.

[7]This ancient ritual is mentioned in Campbell, *Witchcraft and Second Sight*, p. 231, and in *Cape Breton's Magazine*, Number 2, p. 11. Although he does not mention it, the custom must also have existed in Cape Breton when Charles W. Dunn conducted his research there since the issue of *Cape Breton's Magazine* cited contains an interview with an informant who recalled the circling of the house in the direction of the sun ('deiseal'), and the sheepskin attire, all recorded in Cape Breton in 1973.

Chapter 6

[1]Far from being peculiar to the Codroy Valley or to the Scots in Newfoundland, the controlling of children's behaviour by verbal threats of this kind is found in many Newfoundland settlements. See John D.A. Widdowson, *If You Don't Be Good*, Social and Economic Studies No. 21 (St. John's: Institute of Social and Economic Research, Memorial University of Newfoundland, 1977).

[2]Donald A. MacKenzie, *Scottish Folklore and Folk Life Studies in Race, Culture and Tradition* (London and Glasgow: 1935), p. 208.

[3]MacEdward Leach, "Celtic Tales from Cape Breton," in W. Edson Richmond (ed.), *Studies in Folklore* (Bloomington: Indiana University Press, 1957), pp. 40-54.

[4]Carmichael, *Carmina Gadelica*, vol. 3, pp. 352-53.

[5]This tune, though unnamed, is very similar to "Back o' Benachie," with parts 1 and 2 reversed. Syllables are approximate; transcribed by Peter Cooke.

[6]This sounds very much like "Uamh Fhraing," and as such may indicate a memory of the cave of that name on the Isle of Eigg, the island next to the MacArthurs' native Isle of Canna. Uamh Fhraing was referred to as "the massacre cave," as legend has it that the population of that small island took refuge there from a raiding party of MacLeods. Their hiding place was discovered, and the MacLeods were said to have lit a huge fire at the mouth of the cave which smoked them all to death.

[7]The MacArthurs were hereditary pipers to the MacDonalds of the Isles, and tradition has it that the last of these MacArthur pipers went to Canada.

Chapter 7

[1] *Census of Newfoundland and Labrador,* 1901, 1911, 1921 *(JHA).*

[2] Apart from her skill as a craftswoman, Lucy Cormier was an outstanding tradition bearer among the French. She had a wealth of songs which I recorded, along with invaluable historical information from her husband, George, of Upper Ferry.

[3] Sometimes they used two old doors supported by trestles as a milling table. A typical structure was about fifteen feet long, and had benches.

[4] *A'Choiris-Chiuil: The St. Columba Collection of Gaelic Songs* (Glasgow, n.d.), p. 2.

[5] John Ramsay, *Scotland and Scotsmen in the Eighteenth Century,* ed. A. Allardyce (Edinburgh & London: 1888), Vol. 2, p. 410.

[6] In John MacPherson's *An Auanaire* (Edinburgh: MacLachlan and Stewart, 1868), p. 103-04, there is a text entitled "Luinneag" which is very similar in theme, chorus vocables and rhyme scheme to this song.

[7] The tune for "Oran an Tombaca" actually appears untitled in Kenneth Peacock's *Songs of Newfoundland Outports* (Ottawa: National Museums of Canada, 1965), p. 790. He noted that it is a "rather rare example of a song used to accompany the rolling of folding of the cloth after the actual milling process is finished." He adds, however, that he was unfortunately "unable to get the text for this song." It seems extremely unlikely that his informant, Allan MacArthur, could have sung *only* the melody for the recording, for not only were words and tune inseparable, but even the actions were a very integral part of the performance. Perhaps Peacock's comment was due to the fact that there is no available printed text for this song, and transcription only possible with assistance from a literate Gaelic speaker. Any time I recorded milling songs in the Valley out of the context of the actual milling frolic, the singers usually held a sweater or tablecloth and continuously 'milled' with their hands while they sang.

[8] John Lorne Campbell and Francis Collinson (eds), *Hebridean Foklsongs: A Collection of Waulking Songs by Donald MacCormich from 1893* (Oxford: The Clarindon Press, 1969), pp. 15-15.

[9] Francis Tolmie collected this song from Mary Ross of Skye in 1900. It is published in *The Old Songs of Skye: Frances Tolmie and her Circle* (London: Routledge & Kegan Paul, 1977), p. 89.

[10] Familiar to Scots the world over, this song is generally sung in Scots and not English. Since Gaelic-speakers do not usually speak Scots, however, the pronounciation of most of the words in this version is closer to standard English—they simply didn't sing "braw bricht moonlicht nicht," but it is interesting that they had more verses to it than most Scottish peole have ever heard.

[11] Peacock, *Songs of Newfoundland Outports,* p. 366.

[12] Several versions are printed in Stan Hugill's *Shanties from the Seven Seas* (London, 1961), pp. 182-89.

There can be few scholars on either side of the Atlantic who succeed in combining such a wide range of skills as Margaret Bennett. A folksinger of great sensitivity and versatility, she is undoubtedly one of the major figures of the modern Scottish revival; yet at the same time she has to her credit an enviable record of solid ethnological scholarship. I cordially commend this book for its imaginative sympathy, as well as for its erudition.

Hamish Henderson

The traditions that have come down to us of the Gaelic diaspora of the 18th and 19th century rarely mention Newfoundland. Only in a few anecdotes, attributable to sailors and other travellers, are there hints that a Gaelic community once flourished in that remote land. And since our information was confined to these tantalisingly vague and brief reports, it simply never occurred to us that Gaelic in Newfoundland might actually have survived into our own times. Margaret Bennett's book has changed all that.

By an extraordinary stroke of good fortune, Margaret, with a family background in the Isle of Skye, went on holiday to Newfoundland, stayed to take a postgraduate degree in folklore under the redoubtable Herbert Halpert, and met the last remaining Gaels of the Codroy Valley. As her story makes all too clear, it was already past the eleventh hour for their community culture. Yet in the person of Allan MacArthur she found the vital link in a chain of Gaelic tradition that led back to the lands of Clanranald in Scotland. The name of Margaret Bennett and the names of that MacArthur family on whom Margaret's work was focussed are now assured of an honoured place in the history of the Gaels in Canada.

Dr. John MacInnes
[Gaelic scholar, writer and broadcaster]